Take Back the Land

Land, Gentrification, and the Umoja Village Shantytown

Max Rameau

Take Back the Land:
Land, Gentrification, and the Umoja Village Shantytown
By Max Rameau

Copyright © 2008 Max Rameau. All Rights Reserved.

This edition © 2012 AK Press (Edinburgh, Oakland, Baltimore)

ISBN: 978-1-84935-088-4
e-ISBN: 978-1-939202-00-0
Library of Congress Control Number: 2012916902

AK Press	AK Press UK
674-A 23rd Street	PO Box 12766
Oakland, CA 94612	Edinburgh EH8 9YE
USA	Scotland
www.akpress.org	www.akuk.com
akpress@akpress.org	ak@akedin.demon.co.uk

The above addresses would be delighted to provide you with the latest AK Press distribution catalog, which features several thousand books, pamphlets, zines, audio and video recordings, and gear, all published or distributed by AK Press. Alternately, visit our websites to browse the catalog and find out the latest news from the world of anarchist publishing:
www.akpress.org | www.akuk.com
revolutionbythebook.akpress.org

Printed in the United States recycled, acid-free paper.

Cover design by Tim Simons | www.frontgroupdesign.com
Interior by Kate Khatib | www.manifestor.org/design

Take Back the Land:
www.TakeBacktheLand.org | takebacktheland@gmail.com

Max Rameau | afrimax@takebacktheland.org

Contents

This work is dedicated to my wonderful partner Bernadette, our children Serge and Akinle, and to the ancestors who sacrificed for and guide us.

View of Umoja Village from the
parking lot.

Staking a claim on the land.

Delivering housing and a message.

*All photos photos courtesy of
NoelleTheard.com except where noted.*

Preface

ON OCTOBER 23, 2006, at approximately 3:00PM, a coalition of activists, local residents and homeless individuals liberated a vacant lot on the corner of 62nd Street and NW 17th Avenue, in the Liberty City section of Miami.

Over the course of six months, up to fifty-three people at one time, and over 150 people in total, were housed and fed in an urban shantytown situated in the United States.

For six months, formerly homeless people not only found a place to sleep, but a place to call home. They voted on the rules of the community in which they lived and partook in its development and maintenance, cooking and cleaning, and built shanties, a shower, a library and a welcome center. Some used the physical safety and food security to gather their thoughts and save money before moving up and on to an apartment or other living arrangements. Several residents became clean, returned to school or found employment, while living on the land.

Neighbors of the Village first gawked, then donated goods from their own meager belongings, volunteered their time and even broke bread and ate with the residents. Supporters from across the state, and beyond, came to visit, help and show solidarity. Students volunteered in droves, re-igniting a level of student activism not seen in decades.

A sense of ownership and community—call it self-determination—organized a segment of the population widely considered unorganizable.

Virtually all who lived there or visited will attest: the Umoja Village Shantytown was something special.

Umoja Village was part living protest, part street theater and part solution to the problem. It was part militant, part loving. It was simultaneously the most and the least radical response to a disturbing crisis. It was history, yet, the Umoja Village was but a continuation of previous historic acts and trends.

On April 26, 2007, just three days after celebrating its six month anniversary—during which an ambitious program to consolidate living arrangements on the land and attack the vestiges of gentrification were announced—the Umoja Village burned to the ground when a fire started under circumstances that can only be described as suspect.

While the physical structures burned and fell, the sense of community and empowerment that we built can never be destroyed. Umoja—the Swahili word for 'unity'—will rise again.

While land struggles are generally considered the domain of the Third World, devolving material conditions in the United States compel social scientists to examine this strategy for its use in the "first world."

This book, then, is part history of the Umoja Village and part political theory around land struggle and other campaigns that strike at the heart of the power relationship between the poverty of working class African people and the opulence of the wealthiest society in the history of planet Earth.

Hopefully, some of the insights gained—the hard way—will make the road forward clear for those coming to finish the job.

1. The Morning After

A SPLASH OF SUN woke me and, for a brief moment, I was disoriented, wondering why I was in my car at the break of day. I sat up, peered out of the car window and achieved instant and total recall.

To my left were the telephone poles that had been donated three months ago. Most were used to frame our garden beds, but last night the remainder were used as bedding for those who remained to defend the land. Some bodies stretched, preparing to face the day, while others hid under blankets, evading reality, prolonging the inevitable. News trucks were everywhere with a few reporters pacing to and fro, awaiting their live shots.

Mostly, though, there were the charred remains of a devastating fire. The soot, charcoal and ash was punctured by the occasional bright colored shirt or other item that managed to escape the flames. Continuously, smoke rose from the earth, from the smoldering remains of shanties, clothing, papers, food and furniture.

I surveyed the damage from the edge of the burnt section of the lot and thought, "this looks like a disaster." Not until weeks later, looking at photographs and video of the same scene, did I realize that it was not "like a disaster," it was an actual disaster.

I checked in with Bernadette, my partner, and we sketched out a plan for the day. Before hanging up, she handed the phone to our son so I could wish him a happy birthday. The Umoja Village Shantytown burned to the ground on Akinle's first birthday, April 26, 2007.

After greeting our residents and supporters, I organized the setup of new living spaces and the preparation and distribution of breakfast, and tried to jump start the rebuilding process.

News trucks from virtually every local station were parked on the land, poking around, doing live shots and conducting interviews. The residents laughed at our new skyline, courtesy of the media outlets. We joked about hurling our raw food up in the air and having it fall to our plates as fully cooked meals, thanks to the power of the microwave antennas rising from the trucks.

Shortly after 7:00AM the Miami city manager, Pete Hernandez, arrived. After reiterating that our primary desire was for the city to refrain from raiding us, we provided him a brief list of our needs, including portable toilets to replace those melted in the fire. The toilets arrived less than two hours later. Even if temporary, the move demonstrated the extent to which we were an institution in this town and how even officials hostile to our existence were forced to acknowledge and deal with us.

My phone would not stop ringing, even as I tried to manage the steady stream of volunteers, media requests and police interactions all while comforting people who lost their homes and belongings to the fire.

The rebuilding stalled as we ran into one nagging problem after the next in our doomed attempts to purchase construction materials. It was as if the media, city officials and police were in full motion and we were still in a haze. We searched for someone to rent a pickup truck and re- trieve the materials for the hexayurts, our next generation of shanties. Those with licenses were already on runs for food, clothing, tables, chairs and other things. Others who were up all night after the fire were sent home to rest up for the afternoon rebuilding shift. One option after the next fell through, until I finally called Bernadette at home so that she could take charge of the hexayurt purchases.

She was already busy sending e-mails, fielding calls and informing sup- porters about the overnight events, while caring for our Akinle.

The combination of preparing Akinle while fielding calls and sending e-mails meant she did not leave to rent the truck until after 9:00AM, by which time the mood of the police had already changed. The rental place was out of pickups, so Bernadette rented a moving van. She came to pick up Rebecca, who is in charge of our construction and knew exactly which materials to purchase, but they quickly realized the truck had a steering problem, and, consequently, returned to the rental place to exchange the van for a working vehicle.

As police activity picked up, I called Bernadette to find out how close they were to arriving with the materials. When she told me they were back at the rental place, well after 10:00AM, reality struck.

Up until that time, I was in denial about the fact that the Village was gone, focusing instead on the exciting challenge associated with rebuilding from scratch. As I watched the police position themselves around the property, it suddenly hit me that Umoja Village might be gone for good.

THE POLICE MAKE THEIR MOVE

While the number of our supporters on site was not yet significant, by 9:00AM a steady stream of additional police positioned themselves strategically around the land. The overnight police shift seemed sympathetic to our position, allowing us back on the land around 2:00AM with assurances they were under no orders to keep us off the property.

This new crew, by contrast, featured a suspiciously high percentage of black cops, both in charge and on the ground. In fact, it seemed as if they moved all of the white and Latino cops off the land and replaced them with black ones, while doubling the total size of the force. This was an indicator that they were planning to make an aggressive move, but sought to avoid the visual of white cops moving black people off land in the black community.

There was a great deal to manage as residents asked pertinent questions about the pace of rebuilding and the new living arrangements. The media was requesting interviews, including one TV reporter who was both aggressive and seemingly hostile to the very existence of the shantytown. Supporters trickled in, but we had relatively little for them to do, given the fact that we had no rebuilding materials.

The earnest attempt to dislodge us from the land began when police, without notice or discussion, ordered all cars, including media trucks, off the lot. I approached the cop in charge, Major Brown—the same Major Brown who tried to kick us off the land when we first arrived there on

October 23, the black face sent out to do the dirty work. He stated that the cars and people would have to move in order to facilitate a cleanup.

The portion of the lot on which the cars were parked was unaffected by the fire. I argued for our right to remain and he assured us there would be "no bulldozers" or attempts to permanently remove residents from the land. When questioned about the cleanup plan, and the lack of our inclusion in the discussions about the plans, Brown clammed up. His silence was far more revealing than his words.

We gathered to assess our collective emotional state and will to stand up to the coming attack. The residents wanted to defend their homes, but a few had outstanding legal issues which prevented them from doing so. Getting arrested while on probation can result in punishments far disproportionate to the offense, even for those ultimately judged not guilty. Some did not want to be found by abusive former partners or otherwise could not afford an arrest. Others remained at the homeless shelter, where they had been transported in the dark of the night, just a few hours prior. The end result was that a relatively small number of our residents—about ten in all—were able to participate in active defense of their own land, even as others wanted to do so.

HALTING SOCIAL MOVEMENTS

After the powerful social justice movements of the 1960s and 70s, particularly the Black Power movement, the system appears to have adjusted by intentionally devising means to reduce the number of people willing and able to participate in political actions.

During that era, the masses participated in campaigns, including arrestable civil disobedience and direct action. In response, the system conjured ways to deplete the pool of willing and able participants, particularly among the most disaffected and militant segments of society, who also represented the greatest threat to the status quo—the black working class.

Doling out a certain number of cushy jobs and creating other economic conflicts of interest, eliminated a particular class of activists. Others are precluded from participating in actions through the so-called "criminal justice system."

According to the U.S. Commission on Civil Rights, the U.S. inmate population in 1972 stood at approximately 330,000. In 2007, the wealthiest society in the history of the planet incarcerated just over two million people, not including those awaiting trial, on parole or on probation. The

U.S., always eager to proclaim its status as the beacon of freedom, incarcerates 702 people for every 100,000 of its population, compared to 139, 116, 91 and 85 respectively for England, Canada, Germany and France.

But do not limit the comparison to economically developed Western European countries, compare the incarceration rates of every other country on earth: the United States imprisons more people, per capita, than any other country in the world. It is no accident that a disproportionate number of those arrested and incarcerated are black.

Not surprisingly, the increased arrests are coupled with ongoing "tough on crime" policies resulting in longer sentences and harsher parole/probation terms, including harsher punishments for even minor violations. Study after study has scientifically demonstrated, however, that "tough on crime" policies do not result in less crime.

This is no place to advocate conspiracy theories by pointing out the fact that the record high U.S. incarceration rates were not in response to record high crime rates, instead coinciding neatly with record low crime rates, a contradiction if ever there was one. However, one would be remiss in failing to note the modern "tough on crime" era coincided with the surge against the Black Panther Party and other political organizations in the early 1970s.

Not only can authorities seek to arrest activists on a growing list of crimes, with those arrests motivated by, even if technically unrelated to, their political work; but the increased arrests and penalties, particularly on parole or probation violations, make participation in progressive political movements a risky proposition.

While many are willing to take an arrest and spend a few days in jail for a worthy cause, a probation violation could, instead, result in months or even years of jail time for a minor, even principled, offense. Worse still, punishment for probation violations are often not based upon criminal convictions, or finding of guilt, but based upon the arrest itself, something that can happen to anyone, guilty or innocent.

Nonetheless, several residents and supporters prepared to take arrests in defense of their land. It was moving when the residents, many of them elderly, stepped up and offered themselves in sacrifice. John Cata was particularly eloquent and adamant about his right to the land. Cata found a chair, sat down and then proceeded to chain himself to a small table, refusing to leave his home.

THE TROJAN HORSE

Obviously, we preferred to rebuild, but they were planning to come after us, so we prepared accordingly.

The police gathered briefly before breaking to surround the land, posting at each corner, plus in spots in between. They attempted to intimidate us by "asking" us off the land, as opposed to ordering us off, but only a few fell for that one, as twenty-five or so stood our ground, a number that grew and shrunk as allies arrived and police tricks and orders became sharper.

However, after conducting a TV interview, I turned and immediately noticed our numbers on the land were significantly depleted as several residents were lured to the parking lot of the apartment complex next door.

Patty Macias was an early supporter and participant of Take Back the Land and the Umoja Village, having attended most of the initial planning meetings. She was a member of Brothers of the Same Mind and LIFFT, while running her own 501(c)3 organization, Hope for the Homeless, and she participated in virtually every activity to which she was invited, regardless of its political orientation. The problem was that she would, essentially, help the Hatfields one day, only to provide assistance to the McCoys the next, each under the guise of the work of God.

At one of the initial planning meetings, Patty apologized for her tardiness, explaining that she volunteered at a health care event organized by Miami Mayor Manny Diaz. We were floored that she was propping up our biggest political enemy in the morning, only to speed over to a meeting in the afternoon where we not only bashed him, but where our big action directly implicated him in many ways. She was fully vested in both sides of the fence.

In the end, because she cares deeply about the poor and downtrodden, at least on one level, we believed that at some point she would make the connection between the conditions people endured and the policies and politicians who benefited from, and therefore maintained, those conditions. But Ms. Patty remained oblivious to the cause and effect of politics.

So, it was not a great surprise to see our residents gathered around none other than Ms. Patty in the parking lot of the neighboring apartment building. She shouted "come get your t-shirts" to people who just lost their homes, and their t-shirts, to a devastating fire. The system conspired to play on people's losses and financial insecurities in order to lure them off the land. Needless to say, when the residents, brand new t-shirts in hand, tried to re-enter the land, they were met by police securing yellow tape on the neighbors' fence. The tag team worked perfectly.

While there is room in the movement for a broad range of supporters and volunteers, we learned the hard way that there must be some level of ideological or political unity.

We did not fail to recognize the contradiction of someone working on both sides, but we reached a twofold analysis of the problem: first, we believed Patty was well-intentioned and attributed her positioning to naivety and lack of political clarity, a problem common among our people of good will, rather than to her being an agent. Second, we believed her involvement in an overtly political movement would solve the naivety, compelling her to adopt a more rigorous analysis of the political reality, thus "flipping" her to a more progressive political position.

The analysis was fatally flawed. First, intentions are a subjective, not objective, measure of one's actions. I cannot afford to make subjective judgments as to the motivation of the robber in my home. Is he robbing me personally or was I randomly selected? Does he have a drug habit or is this to feed his children or pay medical bills? Is this just a robbery or is he capable of violence? While each consideration is valid in the broader context, at the moment, I just gotta get this fool out of my house.

In the same way, we allowed, in some position of leadership, someone working with and for the gentrification mayor. While the specific motivations matter in certain contexts, in others they are irrelevant. Given her relationship to Manny Diaz, she should not have been allowed into the inner circle.

Secondly, while "flipping" our people to clear and good political positions is an important part of our work, it is no endeavor on which to embark in the middle of a high-stakes contest. Our every action and inaction impacted the lives of scores of individuals, and the fate of a movement. This was no time to try to convert flunkies. We made a tremendous error, and that error just lured our residents off the land. As of this writing, Patty continues to take money out of her own pocket to help the homeless. She also works for the Liberty City Trust, a City of Miami agency. My guess is that the moment her strategic value to the city expires, so will her employment.

SEND IN THE CLOWNS

Yellow tape surrounded the land, forcing most of our residents and supporters onto the sidewalk. The cops looked ready to pounce, but held back. The reality was that Umoja Village enjoyed broad support in the community, a fact evinced by the more than one hundred people who spontaneously gathered in support of the land in the middle of a work day.

Given the emotional response to the housing crisis and the level of community support for Take Back the Land's response to that crisis, the cops could not just come in and kick us out, and everyone knew it. Therefore, the powers-that-be had to mitigate the impact of our support. Having already accomplished the initial step of replacing the white cops with black ones, the next step was to cause confusion, thereby dividing community support for Umoja.

Even as police aggressively forbade Umoja residents and supporters from stepping foot on the land, a contingent of ministers suddenly strolled on, completely unobstructed. Technically they represented the Housing Task Force, appointed by City of Miami District 5 Commissioner Michelle Spence-Jones, but their strategic value lay not in their position on a do-nothing board, but in their prominence as black ministers willing to call for the demolition of what remained of the Umoja Village.

Before the system can make a big move with intrinsic racial implications, they find an Uncle Tom or two, or ten, to parade in front of the media, regurgitating the official government line, against the interests of the black community. The city wanted to evict us and bulldoze the charred remains of the Village, but correctly feared the racial divide surely to follow. So, after finding black cops to arrest the black people, they found negro "leaders" willing to sell out their people, and a movement, on camera.

The crew was led by Rev. Richard Dunn. Dunn ran against Spence-Jones for the District 5 seat in a bitter campaign in which she won and he filed suit against her for "stealing" the election. He continued to bad-mouth her at every opportunity he was afforded. The month after Umoja was founded, Dunn spent a night on a Village couch, in solidarity with the residents and in protest against the crisis of gentrification and housing. The following month, in December 2006, during the "Hands Off Umoja" press conference, Dunn blasted Spence-Jones's effort to pass an emergency ordinance designed to outlaw the Village, calling her everything but a child of God. It was a brutal rant that even embarrassed some of the residents.

Sometime after the press conference, the two ran into each other at a holiday party, and, after a few meetings, Spence-Jones was honored to announce that she was appointing Dunn as the chair of her task force. The stated objective of the task force was to "resolve" the Umoja Village "problem."

Rev. Gaston Smith strolled onto the land, called the place a "crime scene" and announced he was there to "do what is right for the residents." When pressed to talk to even one actual resident, Smith refused.

The Housing Task Force itself was an ad-hoc committee assembled to deal with the Umoja Village, and was almost totally quagmired, unable to make decisions for months on end. Yet, somehow, just a few short hours after a fire, and in the midst of all the chaos and confusion associated with the damage, the group managed to meet and cobble together a strongly-worded statement.

While Dunn attributed the lack of casualties suffered to the mercy of God, he evidently did not consider the "miracle" a message from God, urging us to remain and rebuild from the ashes. On behalf of the Task Force, Dunn called for the shutdown of the Village, so that it not be allowed to rise again, there or anywhere else.

The media tossed the Reverends the usual softball questions, so I decided to jump in the game and ask Dunn, and the Task Force, a question:

"Two weeks ago, on April 13th, there was a fire on the 800 block of SW 23rd Avenue in Little Havana, just a few miles from here. The building burned and all residents were made homeless. Are you calling on the city to disallow rebuilding on that land as well?"

Dunn hesitated... and then ended the press conference.

The hypocrisy notwithstanding, the black ministers once again fulfilled what is emerging as their new social role: invoking the name of God in order to imply divine sanction of government action against the black community. The end result is a setback of the nascent political movement and sheer confusion among those who support the liberation and other political movements while simultaneously striving to live according to the wishes of God, as represented by ordained religious figures.

I am reasonably certain that those organizations associated with, or directly employing, those ministers, and others willing to fulfill their vital social role, will be adequately funded in future government appropriation cycles.

With police in position, and the blessing of several prominent black ministers, the city was now prepared to make their move.

THE ARREST-A-FEST

While denying our residents and supporters the luxury, police allowed whites and City of Miami supporters to move on and off the land with impunity. They assumed that any whites in Liberty City must be there on behalf of the city, which turned out to be a poor assumption. The tactic, however, served its purpose by keeping our numbers on the land low, even though we had plenty of supporters lining the sidewalk.

In any event, while I was on the south side of the lot, Amanda Seaton, one of our key organizers, was on the north side informing residents of their rights, as police prevented them from re-entering the land. Amanda explained they had the right to be on the land, just like all of the other people who were on the land and moving on and off without police interference.

For her crimes, Amanda was summarily arrested and charged with an "affray," whatever that is. Months later, upon viewing video of the arrest, prosecutors dropped all charges against her. Getting the charges dropped months after the fact was great, but the intended damage was done—the residents did not broach the yellow tape, understanding that whites could cross it but they could not.

We complained about the selective enforcement of the no trespassing order, and with the help of the ACLU and others, were able to get a few of our people onto the land.

But Amanda was in custody and the police were not letting Mamyrah Prosper, another key organizer, through, so we were down two of our organizers. Power U, the Miami Workers Center and the Lake Worth Kids stepped up big, picking up the decision making where needed.

For a few hours that morning, individuals from separate organizations, and some from no organization at all, thought and operated as one solitary unit. People made decisions autonomously and embraced full ownership over the land and our defense of it.

Decision making was seamless, even if hectic, and offered a glimpse into what movement-based direct action might look like, in the midst of a hot political battle.

The Workers Center was moving chants, Power U secured tables and chairs, the Lake Worth Kids planned direct actions and Bernadette headed the legal team.

The police huddled and gestured, preparing their move. Most of the media went to interview elected officials at the Miami City Commission meeting, leaving us with little media cover.

In the meantime, the weather started threatening and with several elderly residents, as well as some open food, clothes and other items, we decided to set up a tent for the residents.

Tony Romano of the Miami Workers Center opened the tent and before he could connect the first poles, the police swooped in and arrested him. I already had two rods in hand and as soon as I touched them together, I was arrested.

Once in the police car, I saw Mamyrah stuck outside of the yellow tape. With me and Amanda locked up and Mamyrah on the sidewalk, the core of Take Back the Land was off of the land. However, with Power U, the Miami Workers Center and our other supporters, I was fully confident in the movement's ability to handle the situation.

DOING HARD TIME

Tony and I were walked into the police station, where Amanda sat alone in the holding cell. She was thrilled to see another soul and at the prospect of getting an update.

After a minute or so, Commander Whitehead walked in the cell and asked me to step out, as he and the Miami Community Relations Board wanted to talk. We sat in an office cubicle and I was given yet another unique explanation as to why we were moved from the land. The conversation was open and honest, but, given the circumstances, untimely.

I was informed that I only had to sign some papers to be released, but I asserted that I had to share the fate of everyone else arrested. Therefore, if they were unable to release everyone else, I wanted to go to jail as well. They agreed to free everyone.

When I left the holding cell, there were two people, but I returned to find six. Before getting an update myself, I wanted everyone to know what happened in the next room, so I started spilling the beans about the little chat, but was forced to stop when I was called out of the cell again.

It appears there was a "situation" back on the land, so they wanted me to return and help calm things down a bit.

"Um... but I'm under arrest."

Next thing I knew, Commander Whitehead was driving me back to the land. There was a chaotic gathering of people lining the sidewalk while chanting and darting on and off of the land, a scene made difficult to process by the incessant whirring and beeping of the bulldozers actively clearing out the charred remains of our Village.

People were shocked to see me, given the fact that I had just recently been carted away. There must have been two hundred people cramming the sidewalk around the land, chanting down the police and bulldozers. Cops were everywhere watching for protesters attempting to come off the yellow tape. The whirring and beeping of the bulldozers was maddening.

They threatened to bulldoze our food and water, so I ran up to help Bernadette drag a table off the land and onto the sidewalk. She looked over to say thanks and literally did a double take when she recognized me. In the midst of this crazy scene, Bernadette walked up behind me and whispered "is this a conjugal visit?"

Seeing me reassured those concerned about my welfare and had a calming effect that required no effort on my part. I discovered a slew of us had been arrested, including several of the Lake Worth Kids and other anarchists for standing in front of moving bulldozers, and John Cata, who had fallen to the ground while chained to a night stand. Cata had fainted and had been sent to the VA hospital. Denise Perry of Power U had attended to the fallen Cata and been promptly arrested as well. In all, eleven of us were arrested that day.

The crowd was chanting and yelling. It was a powerful, powerful scene.

After a few moments, I approached Whitehead and asked him, "What's up?" He looked around and said things seemed to be calming down a bit, so I rephrased my question. "Am I under arrest?"

"Oh! Right. Hang on right here while I get someone to bring you to the station."

The cop escorting me to the car realized he did not have the keys and asked me to wait as he retrieved them. For several minutes, I stood in the middle of NW 17th Avenue, which was partially closed due to the activity, all alone except for the passing traffic. After a while, one of the officers who had handled my previous arrest in January, when we attempted to liberate vacant units of public housing, approached.

He slowed down and looked confused. "Hi. Max... um, aren't you..."

I spared him the uncomfortable question. "Yeah, I'm under arrest, but they brought me back here, and now the guy bringing me to the station lost his keys. I guess this would be a good time for me to escape, huh?"

He laughed, patting me on the back. "No, no. Don't do that. I'm sure he'll be back. Just wait here."

And there I stood, alone, again, on NW 17th Avenue, partially blocked due to police activity.

I was dropped off at the police station and told the front desk would let me back into the holding cell. As I walked in the front door, I recognized the back of attorney John De Leon, who stood at the window vigorously demanding to see his client. When the police at the window told him I was not there, he just knew he was unearthing a major cover-up. Once back inside the station, my paperwork was ready, so all I had to do was sign and leave. I updated the other arrestees, signed and left, returning to the land.

THE GREAT WALL

Amusing anecdotes aside, the harsh reality is that we no longer controlled the land.

Throughout Umoja's existence, we argued that attributing the housing scandal to government incompetence was a mistake, as high levels of competence were required to steal, lie and cover up as effectively as city and county officials did. For better or for worse, our assumptions were validated as, within hours after the fire, the City of Miami coordinated police activities, hired bulldozer operators and erected a barbed wire fence around the land that the community controlled for six months.

That evening, we rallied on the sidewalk, outside of the new fence, paid for with our tax dollars. Standing against that barbed wire, designed to ensure that no people without homes could use the vacant and publicly-owned land, was an affront to us all.

As the rally came to a close, we huddled, working out meeting times to discuss our next move.

It was hard to believe, but the Umoja Village was gone. The only things that remained were a pile of logs and the wooden Take Back the Land sign.

The residents of Umoja Village were, once again, homeless. We were all tired and uncertain about the next step. We were sure, however, that we were ready to fight to Take Back the Land once again.

The first tents are erected moments
after we arrive on the land.

Poncho negotiates and awaits
word on our fate.

A "pallet palace" shanty shell.

2. Crisis and Corruption

LIKE ELSEWHERE IN THE US, during the early 2000s, South Florida experienced what was promoted as a 'real estate boom.' The boom was facilitated by a number of accelerants, including Federal Reserve manipulation of finance and mortgage rules, paving the way for an exploding sub-prime lending market, thereby increasing the number of buyers and, naturally, the price of the product. More than coincidentally, this artificially manufactured market boom kept the U.S. economy afloat, particularly in the wake of the dot-com bust and the post-September 11 economic slowdown.

The mass media and local governments hyped the rapid rise in real estate values, but for most people, it was irrelevant as an economic or wealth engine. To the contrary, the way this economic trend impacted most people was by increasing their rent or home purchase price.

Ironically, the same market that increased home prices also made it easier to get financing for those overpriced homes, a trade-off which, in the long run, worked to the disadvantage of the poor, and even many struggling to maintain middle class status, as the inflated prices returned to haunt new homeowners in the form of record foreclosures.

The larger point is that while this economic phenomenon was spun as a positive by government officials and the media, the extent to which it impacted the majority of people was not as a boom, but as the driving force behind a crisis of gentrification and affordable housing. Of course, economic trends are not spun based on their impact to the majority, they are spun based on the impact to the rich. The real story, however, was about the crisis, not the boom.

GENTRIFCATION

After months, even years, of work by activists and organizations, the media, local and national, began reporting on gentrification. While gentrification was generally framed as the underbelly of the real estate boom, it is actually more accurate to think of the real estate "boom" as a side effect of gentrification.

In a nutshell, gentrification is the forced removal of the poor, followed by heavy capital investments required to improve the physical conditions of rundown neighborhoods, in order to replace them with wealthier people. The end result is that the wealthier people enjoy renovated housing for less than purchasing new homes and the poor are forced to move to a completely different neglected neighborhood, without improving their condition. All benefits for the rich, none for the poor.

Clearly, gentrification includes an economic aspect, in which the poor are forced out and replaced by the wealthy. In most places, but particularly in the United States, everything has a racial component, and gentrification is no different. In the racial aspect of gentrification, those removed are largely black, or other people of color, and those replacing them are largely white, or at least whiter than those they are replacing.

Additionally, gentrification includes two tracks: residential, displacing individuals from their homes; and commercial, displacing small local businesses and replacing them with larger, heavily capitalized businesses catering to the new residents while making the old ones feel unwelcome, further facilitating their departure.

Gentrification destroys historically black communities, forcing out longtime residents who suffered through the bad times, but do not get to experience the good times that follow the physical improvements of "revitalization."

After years, often decades, of neglect at the hands of government and private capital, the horrendous conditions of abject poverty are used to justify an influx of public and private dollars to upgrade living conditions.

The bad part is that instead of eliminating poverty, or the conditions thereof, these 'urban renewal' programs simply move poor people from one underserved community to another. In the end, millions of dollars are mobilized in the name of fighting poverty, but instead of improving conditions for the poor, it moves the poor out of their neighborhoods in order to provide subsidized housing for the middle class or the wealthy.

During the 1990s, as South Florida's population swelled, the low-income housing stock proved insufficient, marking the beginning of the crisis of gentrification and housing. Instead of detailing the numerous factors that triggered gentrification in South Florida, the focus here is on instances of direct government sponsorship of gentrification.

During such a crisis, most expect the government and its housing agencies to intervene by increasing the number of low-income housing units. In South Florida, however, local governments responded to the crisis by actively decreasing the number of low-income housing units.

Most are reluctant to believe that officials would or could do such a thing, so here are some examples of what they did and how.

HOPE VI

In 1999, Miami-Dade County submitted a federal HOPE VI application, proposing the demolition of the 850 row houses that made up the Scott and Carver housing projects in unincorporated Miami-Dade, just west of the City of Miami boundaries. Even as they proclaimed their intentions to rebuild them and make life better for the residents, red flags were flying all over the place.

In the first place, Miami-Dade Housing Agency (MDHA), which administers public housing and the local implementation of the HOPE VI program, was fresh off a legal settlement in which they admitted to intentionally steering blacks into dilapidated public housing units while offering whites and Hispanics newer units or coveted housing vouchers, which can be used to pay rent for a private house or apartment. It was a bit challenging to accept that the same agency that was actively discriminating against us last year was now ready to make good faith amends via HOPE VI.

Intentions aside, another problem was the simple math. The Miami-Dade Board of County Commissioners (BCC) ignored widespread resident opposition to the plan and voted to displace the over three thousand overwhelmingly black residents in order to demolish 850 units of very low-income public housing, replacing it with eighty(!) units of public housing and 462 units in all. Obviously, only eighty of the units were sufficiently subsidized to meet the needs and financial situations of most Scott-Carver residents, who were, after all, in public housing.

Even if each of the 462 housing units were filled with former Scott-Carver residents, the BCC vote still resulted in a net loss of almost four hundred homes. But the reality is that only eighty units were intended for low-income people, and in all probability, the vast majority of those eighty would not be the black people who suffered the horrid conditions that the slumlord County maintained in the Scott-Carver homes.

The $106 million in HOPE VI money, made available precisely because of the abject poverty suffered by the residents, was not even used to alleviate that abject poverty, but, instead, to subsidize housing for the middle class.

The County neither proposed nor intended to use those funds to end poverty. Sure, they used the funds to solve some physical manifestations of poverty, by tearing down old buildings and constructing new ones. However, while such actions might help inanimate objects such as concrete, metal, glass, wiring and pipes escape poverty, the actions do not, in and of themselves, help human beings escape poverty.

The poor at Scott's are forcibly removed from their own (dilapidated) homes, and condemned to relive those same abject conditions in another locale, possibly one with fewer family and social safety nets. Sure, new homes are built, but they are built primarily and overwhelmingly for people who are not poor.

This represents the redistribution of wealth in the most perverse way possible, taking from the very poor in order to contract rich politically-connected developers into building housing for the middle class.

Additionally, the intentional and government-sponsored dislocation of over three thousand residents from a historically black community effectively gerrymanders the meager political power base black people managed to build over time. Whatever political power black communities have yet to gain, the little power we have cannot be grown or even maintained if the people are made even more economically and politically unstable by government-sponsored gentrification.

Under any similar circumstance, serious questions should be raised about back room dealings associated with the forced removal of thousands of people from a community primed for redevelopment. Those questions are even more pointed when the elected official advocating for the removal of his own voting bloc is, himself, black.

District 2 County Commissioner Dorrin Rolle is black and "represents"—in the loosest application of the term imaginable—the Liberty City community which was home to Scott-Carver, and the primary proponent behind the plan gutting his district of voters, surely replacing them with a non-black middle class unlikely to re-elect him.

Not surprisingly, when Rolle campaigns, few contributions come from the district he represents. Most come from his real constituency: wealthy developers with business ties with the County, including projects on which Rolle votes.

Officials like Rolle are well compensated for selling poor black people down the river. If Rolle were fighting for the black community, instead of fighting to destroy it, he surely would have been indicted by now. However, given his role as the grinning black face on a racist plan to move poor blacks out to make room for wealthier and whiter people, he is safe from prosecution, regardless of how much money he rakes in on the side or how poorly he mismanages the social service agency he is highly overcompensated to direct.

In the meantime, the clear objective of the HOPE VI program, in Miami-Dade and across the US, is to use the cover of fighting poverty to mobilize millions of dollars to facilitate the gentrification of strategically-situated black communities. In spite of its stated objective—revitalizing public housing—this is a program which should never see the light of day again.

PUBLIC HOUSING VACANCIES

In late 2003, public housing residents noticed a growing number of vacancies in their developments. It appeared as if every time a family moved out of a unit, MDHA would quickly board it up rather than occupy it with a needy family from the sizable housing assistance wait list.

The rise in vacancies was more than just anecdotal. According to the Michigan-based Mackinac Center for Public Policy, the standard federal HUD vacancy rate is 3 percent. By contrast, in 2004 over 10 percent of the County's 11,000 or so units of public housing sat vacant, during an affordable housing crisis in which over 39,000 families languished on the housing assistance wait list. The Miami Workers Center and the group they formed, Low-Income Families Fighting Together (LIFFT), took note and initiated the Fill the Vacancies campaign.

MDHA initially denied the vacancy rate was abnormal. Then, with the same mouths they use to kiss their mothers, boldly asserted that the reason so many public housing units sat vacant was because MDHA was fighting against racial discrimination. If only they were joking.

In settling the discrimination lawsuit against it the year prior, MDHA promised to stop racial segregation in housing placement. In an extraordinary leap of imagination, application of logic and display of dogged political will, officials argued that filling the vacancies expeditiously would, ultimately, result in moving black people into majority black public housing projects. According to MDHA, such an act is tantamount to racist housing practices, and MDHA will not—dammit—engage in racist housing practices. They used the cover of fighting racism to advance their racist agenda of vacating housing units at the expense of poor black people.

The real problem, of course, was not that black people lived in the same neighborhood as other black people, the problem is that Miami-Dade County is a slumlord. The real remedy to the problem of moving blacks into slums is not to move blacks next door to whites or Latinos, it is compelling the County to stop being a slumlord. In lieu of that, the County decided to keep units vacant and families homeless, invoking the fight against racism along the way.

After months of wrangling, during which the story became a media nuisance, the BCC voted to give $1.5 million to MDHA to fill the vacancies.

Before the funds were granted, there were 1,200 public housing vacancies in the county inventory. After the money was spent the number of vacancies increased to a total of 1,800. It remains unclear how the money was spent, and the elected officials of the BCC are not asking.

MIAMI'S PRIVATE APARTMENTS

Starting in 1998, the City of Miami purchased a number of privately-owned slums along 62nd, 61st and 60th Streets, between NW 12th and 17th Avenues. The city notoriously overpaid the slumlords for their units and quickly evicted the tenants.

After a number of protests, the city signed contracts with tenants from each of the 482 demolished units, granting the right to return to equally affordable housing, once rebuilt. Of course, the units were never rebuilt.

The city, through the Model City Trust, spent $8.5 million, but somehow failed to rebuild even one single unit through 2007.

One of the demolished buildings was located on the corner of 62nd Street and NW 17th Avenue in Liberty City, the same lot upon which the Umoja Village was built. Oh, the irony.

At the end of 2006, in response to the Village, the City of Miami released an RFP offering each of those lots to developers for free, so long as they could prove they had enough cash on hand to begin building housing—not even low-income housing—in the next three months. For free.

It is not difficult to see, then, how Liberty City was the only section of Miami-Dade that lost population between 1990 and 2000, at a time when the County's population was otherwise booming.

THE CRA

Chapter 162 of the Florida State Statutes allows for the creation of Community Redevelopment Agencies (CRAs) in poor areas explicitly to alleviate "blight" and "slum" by reinvesting captured property tax increments.

While the law is generally flexible, a few things are mandated, including a written Community Redevelopment Plan. The only tangible objective of the Plan is to "provide for the development of affordable housing in the area." If no affordable housing is built, the Plan must "state the reason" why no housing is being built by a CRA whose primary purpose is to build housing. (F.S. 163.360 S. 2(c)).

In the midst of the most severe housing crisis and scandal in the US, Miami-Dade County and the City of Miami, both of which failed to find money to build low-income housing, are breaking their necks to fund three big projects: a retractable dome stadium for a professional sports franchise that already has a stadium, a parking lot for a swanky performing arts center and an underground tunnel leading from I-395 directly to the Port of Miami (in a city that rises just five to twenty feet above sea level).

The Carnival Center for the Performing Arts (CCPA) opened twenty months behind schedule and almost $200 million over budget in a county crying broke when asked for economic development or housing money.

In spite of the fact that it is clearly not affordable housing, the CCPA continues to receive $1.43 million per year from the CRA. If that makes you happy, you will be downright giddy to learn to that the CCPA was built without any parking spaces. The local powers and media were so eager to open the world-class arts center that they won't even investigate an obvious scam (suggested title: 'Opera House of Lies'). After $446 million, there are no arrests, no investigations and no parking spaces.

Separately, a plan to build an underground tunnel to allow cargo trucks to bypass downtown traffic and connect directly to the Port of Miami is in the final planning stages, with a preliminary price tag of $1 billion.

We can only hold hands and pray that this project is not managed by the same people who built the CCPA.

In the face of massive housing agency scandals and demands for more low-income housing, County Commissioners displayed no sense of shame, declining to even replace the money stolen from housing programs. In the City of Miami, Mayor Manny Diaz trudges forth undaunted in his quest to reduce poverty by removing all poor people from the City limits, replacing them with yuppie condo dwellers.

This is the context under which the CRA, whose board is comprised of the City of Miami Commissioners, is poised to divert millions of dollars from the poor to fund a retractable dome stadium, parking for wealthy patrons of the CCPA and an underwater tunnel to ensure the speedy delivery of products the poor residents of the CRA cannot even afford.

Because neither the port nor the tunnel are, technically, in the CRA boundaries, the CRA board plans to redraw the boundaries to ensure that the diversion of funds from the poor to the inane is legal, even if not moral.

The lesson is that when politicians really want something, they find the political will and the money. Conversely, there are pots of money specifically set aside to build low-income housing, but politicians do not want to build that housing. Whether through the CRA or other agencies, the officials take money from the poor, drive it through the underwater tunnel and deliver it to the center for the performing rich.

GOVERNMENT ROLE IN GENTRIFICATION

Reaction to these real-life stories is often one of disbelief. "I don't understand why they can't fill those vacancies." "Do they know that money is supposed to go to build housing?" "I can't believe they haven't rebuilt Scott Projects."

Particularly given the rate of gentrification and the severity of the housing crisis, to many, the actions of government officials defy logic.

Such logic, however, rests on the assumption that one of the roles of the government is to build low-income housing for those ignored by the market. During a housing crisis, government agencies presumably mitigate the crisis by providing more housing. When such housing is not provided, the logic continues, it is the result of either incompetence or corruption, a problem resolved by ridding the bureaucracy of the incompetent or corrupt individuals.

This logical set presumes the job of government is to serve the interests of the citizenry in general and, in this instance, poor black women, in particular. Both the premise and, therefore, its logical conclusion are false.

The job of local government is not to serve the interests of regular people, much less poor black women; it is to serve the interests of big business, such as wealthy developers.

As gentrification ravaged entire communities, the housing crisis spiraled out of control and the housing scandal exploded, the powers-that-be and the mass media encouraged the notion that incompetence and corruption were at fault. Nothing could be further from the truth. While there clearly was, and is, corruption, the crisis is a consequence of the government housing policy, not an impediment to its implementation. Elected officials and government workers knew exactly what they were doing and how to accomplish their objectives, in an efficient and highly competent manner.

The harsh truth is that Miami-Dade County and the City of Miami did not try to increase the number of low-income housing units and fail; they tried to decrease the number of low-income housing units and succeeded.

The real, albeit unstated, public policy of local governments is to decrease the number of low-income housing units in order to manufacture a severe housing crisis and advance gentrification, resulting in a bonanza for developers who watch their holdings blossom and their investment in local graft return substantial dividends.

SUPPLY AND DEMAND

Imagine a developer builds a large apartment complex in order to profit from low-income rentals. The problem is that while the developer wants to charge $400 per month for each unit, several blocks away, public housing charges a percentage of one's income, a monthly amount ranging from $25 to $300. Short of providing some serious amenities or lowering his prices, the developer will not fill up the complex and profits will remain skimpy.

If, however, the public housing itself were eliminated, its residents would be forced to search for new digs at the mercy of the market, and to the delight of the developer. In addition to generating more tenants, eliminating a significant subset of the low-income housing pool—in this case, 850 units—impacts overall real estate values as well. That is to say, if the supply is manipulated by taking "products" off the shelf and the demand by kicking people out of their homes, prices, and more importantly profits, increase. In the end, not only can the developer charge his full $400 rent, but there is no brake preventing him from charging $800 for the same unit that once struggled to attract tenants at $400.

Make no mistake, these local governments deliberately, intentionally and competently set out to reduce the number of low-income housing units as a means of supporting politically-connected developers, who profiteer from the market manipulation and subsequent housing crisis.

MDHA went to extreme lengths to deny families admittance to vacant public housing units, particularly in the face of community organizations and some media scrutiny. The HOPE VI process was incredibly intricate and complex. The ability to produce false documents and conceal tens of millions of dollars in fraud and thievery in a bureaucracy and over the course of years cannot be accomplished either by a lone crook or a group of amateurs.

Blaming the mess on a "few bad apples," whether incompetent or corrupt, is, in a sense, reassuring, because the dilemma is solved by firing or replacing a few people. Such an explanation, however, lets the system off the hook, diverting attention from the deeper root causes of the housing crisis and onto one or a handful of individuals.

The objective measurable actions of the government, including votes taken openly and on the record, demonstrate that the real, albeit unstated, public policy of at least two governmental bodies was to reduce the number of low-income housing units on the market. Because they were the primary benefactors of these actions, it is reasonable to infer that the public policy, which worked against the interests of those in need of housing, was advanced at the behest of wealthy politically-connected developers, who continue to line the campaign coffers—and pockets—of the elected officials.

As the real estate market turns the corner from cyclical boom to cyclical bust, another opportunity arises to gauge the allegiance of officials. In Miami alone, tens of thousands of condos are set to hit an already slumping market, resulting, in all likelihood, in a tremendous inventory glut, straddling developers with thousands of unprofitable empty apartment units. While the feds, state, county and City of Miami have all drastically reduced vouchers and other assistance to renters, as wealthy developers complain about profits, look for their sponsored elected officials to miraculously find millions of dollars to revive some version of the rental assistance program, not to assist renters, but, instead to bail out the speculators, protecting them from financial losses.

The Fred Hampton House.

The Nelson Mandela House.

The "Liberty Café" community kitchen.

3. Systemic Issues

As the *Miami Herald*'s "House of Lies" exposé hit the stands late in the summer of 2006, longtime housing and anti-gentrification activists felt vindicated. The years of complaining to an unresponsive media—including, incidentally, the *Miami Herald*—about the housing crisis were finally paying off, even if the series itself stopped short of recognizing the work of these same activists and groups.

Nonetheless, three major factors joined to usher in new possibilities for stronger political action on the issue of housing, gentrification and land: first, the crisis of housing and gentrification reached critical mass. The objective conditions were bad and people were already reacting to those conditions. Second, the ongoing consciousness raising, mobilizing and organizing around the issue of housing and gentrification awoke the community to a broader political context, priming people for action. And third, the outrage generated by the exposure of public corruption in the media created the political space required to step up the political action.

Taken together, these factors generated a palpable shift in the political dynamics, both in the black community and—seemingly for the first time—among whites, Latinos and even the Cuban-Americans.

THE MOVEMENT RESPONDS

Public sentiment was hot following the publication of "House of Lies," and the Power U Center for Social Change kicked off the movement's response to the series by calling for and leading an action at the County Government Center. The action included a press conference followed by a speak-out during which victims of the housing crisis would share their stories and express their outrage. The spectacle would, presumably, attract passersby who would listen in and even join the protest.

After an initial reluctance, support for the action grew. Turnout was way better than expected and the message resonated with the homeless living on county property as well as the average person waiting for the bus or conducting some sort of business at or near county hall.

As the speakout began, we received word that several Commissioners were conducting their own press conference, announcing their own action plan in response to the stories. It should come as no surprise that more than a year later no action has been taken on that previously announced plan.

This coincidence, in time, presented us with the golden opportunity to directly confront our tormentors, not just yell at their ghosts in the shadow of the government center. Opportunity made a suggestion and we took the hint.

We scrapped the final part of the rally, and virtually the entire contingent—including many passersby—marched into the Commission press room. As the Commissioners finished their statements to the press, we peppered them with questions of our own. The guiltiest party, District 2 Commissioner Dorrin Rolle, ran for the hills, never to return, leaving the other brave, albeit corruptible, souls to defend him.

They took all kinds of well-earned abuse in the form of rough questioning and harsh criticisms. They were yelled at, called thieves and crooks, and, ultimately, we took over the press room, running them out. It's shameful that Rolle, who was directly responsible for a number of the bad decisions reported in the *Herald* series, was not there to take his lumps as well. It was very telling, however, that Rolle's colleagues defended him to the bitter and humiliating end.

We finished our action from the official county press room. It was inspiring and militant, but most were too angry to be proud or even fully aware of the bravery they displayed by standing toe-to-toe with the powers.

The support for and positive reaction to the action demonstrated, in a concrete way, a shift in public sentiment. The shift was significant and noticeable, and, therefore, worthy of a fresh assessment of conditions on the ground.

THE BIRD'S EYE VIEW

Progressive forces must engage in regular movement-wide assessments of issues and conditions on the ground. These assessments are critical to understanding shifts in long-standing assumptions, emerging weaknesses of our targets and changes in strategies and tactics employed by both the targets and our movement.

Additionally, these assessments, when properly conducted, facilitate the mapping of a "bird's eye view" of the movement on the ground. Because we are so intensely engaged in individual campaigns and programs, a tunnel vision of sorts often takes hold, lulling organizations and activists into perceiving their work as the movement rather than understanding their work as part of a broader movement, together with other organizations, individuals and parts of the movement.

Objective "bird's eye view" assessments can help one social force understand and appreciate the work of others, and how the parts fit and function together in the context of the broader movement. Of course, that same view can just as easily reveal the limitations or outright backwardness of other forces, including those assumed to be close allies, raising difficult questions in the process.

Either way, the "bird's eye view" contextualizes the general direction of the movement in relation to principled goals and objectives; identifies potential openings as well as roadblocks; and helps orient and space different 'parts' of the movement to each other, targets and the principled goals and objectives towards which the movement strives. As such, regular gatherings of movement forces to assess political realities is essential.

The Miami Workers Center not only recognized a shift in conditions on the ground, but the need to assess those conditions and to include some outside of their organization in that assessment. Their assessment would examine changes in public perception and the opening of political space and propose what to do next, given new realities.

It was important for the movement to understand precisely what was happening and not make broad, sweeping assumptions that could falsely color our work. For example, in analyzing press coverage, we concluded that the "House of Lies" series did an excellent job of uncovering specific instances of public corruption by housing agency executives and mid-managers.

However, two important areas were lacking: first, public corruption attributed to elected officials was skimpy and insufficient. While there is no way to know for sure, we speculated the *Herald* utilized a high-ranking government official—probably an assistant county manager—as their own "deep throat" and critical source of information, and that source directed the story line towards specific housing agency officials. By necessity, then, the dropping of crumbs in one direction led the reporter(s) towards bureaucrats by diverting them away from elected officials, for whom the high-ranking housing official worked, even if indirectly.

Second, and more importantly, at no point did the "House of Lies" series question the public policy decisions enacted by local governments, which adversely impacted the crisis at hand. For example, while the series exposed delays, missing families and misspent/stolen money associated with the HOPE VI project at Scott-Carver, framed as the consequence of corruption and incompetence, it deliberately refrained from questioning the wisdom of approving a plan that intentionally eliminated over 750 units of public housing during a low-income housing crisis.

While the series lamented the housing crisis in a general sense, it was oblivious to the most significant factors contributing to the crisis. At publication time, only eleven of the 462 HOPE VI replacement homes were built, even as tens of millions of dollars were gone and unaccounted for. While this is a dramatic expression of the impact of public corruption on the housing crunch, the public policy impact was even greater, but received no mention.

The BCC, egged on by Commissioner Rolle, voted to raze Scott-Carver's 850 units of public housing, replacing them with eighty units of public housing and 462 units in all. The public policy impact of the BCC vote—a net loss of over 750 low-income housing units—was greater than the impact of the corruption, which had resulted, at publication time, in a loss of 80 low-income units and 451 units in all.

One of my high school literature teachers spent far too much energy, or so it seemed at the time, ensuring that his students understood the difference between the 'setting' and the 'theme' of a story. While the setting could happen virtually anywhere—outer space, the wild west, the inner city, the jungles of Africa—a story only took place in the setting, but was not about the setting. The story was about the theme(s). A love story is a love story, whether set in space or in the heart of the city.

Were he to have read them all himself, my guess is that Mr. Dent would have argued that the setting for the "House of Lies" and related stories was the housing crisis, but the theme of the story was not housing, it was public corruption.

In the series and subsequent editorials, the *Herald* expressed neither principled nor strategic concern for the public policy of housing, regardless of how bad, so long as no money was stolen during the implementation of those bad policies. The clear priority of the story was to stop public corruption, not necessarily to end the housing crisis.

Conversely, the major issue and theme for the political movement was gentrification and the housing crisis, and its impact on the human beings in our community.

It was entirely possible, then, that the media would support throwing individual crooks in jail, without pursuing the more fundamental demands of building more housing for poor people. In this scenario, the rich would no longer have their tax money stolen, but poor people would still have no housing. The rich get a much better deal from this solution than the poor, which is understandable, given that the proposal emanates from huge corporate entities still trying to convince us about the benefits of the real estate "boom."

From a public policy perspective, even if all of the stolen and misspent money was returned and then used for the purposes intended by the elected officials, there would still be a severe housing crisis in South Florida because the officials voted to create a severe housing crisis in South Florida.

In a real way, the media switched the subject on us all. The big problem is the housing crisis, but the media shifted focus away from how many housing units are built and destroyed—the bottom line as far as the crisis is concerned—and towards public corruption. This is not to imply that public corruption is not a problem or that is should not be covered, but housing is a problem and that should be covered as well. As such, one of the tasks of the movement would be to shift attention back to the question of housing.

The point here is not to diminish the significance of the "House of Lies" series in particular or the importance of uncovering public corruption in general. Rather, the point is to properly and scientifically deline-ate issues in order to understand precisely where each social force stood in relation to the movement, our demands and related campaigns.

Nonetheless, there is no denying that the series added momentum to the ongoing efforts of several organizations, and presented an opportuni-ty for us to leverage the story to advance the fight for more housing, not just the fight for less stealing. In addition, as the protest at government center demonstrated, the general level of disgust with local governments created greater political space from which we could take more militant actions as a means of advancing our demands.

Conversely, government officials suffered a loss of legitimacy and mor-al high ground. This loss of legitimacy undermined their own well-worn ability to stave off our demands by arguing they are working hard to pro-vide housing for low-income people.

PARTS OF THE MOVEMENT

In terms of the "bird's eye view," the local anti-gentrification movement was shaping up into three separate, but related, parts. As a movement, the members of one part might not agree on the objectives or even strategies and tactics of those operating in another part, but each player could be expected to maximize their impact inside of their own 'part' of the move-ment. The parts, as identified, were:

PUBLIC CORRUPTION.

Everyone was against public corruption, or, at least a certain kind of public corruption. Civic groups, homeowners, and even corporate inter-ests, including the media, were against public corruption not only be-cause it was their tax money being stolen, but because it undermined the illusion that the U.S. is better than all those "Third World Countries," long stereotyped as the exclusive sites of public corruption.

So, while the common interests were very narrow—a specific kind of public corruption—there was widespread support for this part of the movement, and, therefore, we wanted to cultivate and encourage its emergence.

There were, however, two dilemmas inherent in entering the public corruption part of the movement and taking on related campaigns. First, it was possible that, like the media series, all emphasis would be placed on corruption with none placed on the more significant concerns around the public policy of housing. That is to say, a large mobilization could be built around returning the money stolen from the HOPE VI project, but no additional housing units would be built, even though the biggest problem with HOPE VI was not the stealing, but the actual plan itself.

On a related note, if corruption is perceived as the primary reason for the housing crisis, then the public might be easily placated by a few token firings, strategically designed to create the appearance of change, but resulting in no additional homes being built, and, therefore, failing to impact the housing crisis in any concrete way.

County Mayor Carlos Alvarez's response to the crisis epitomized this very concern. With great fanfare, Alvarez shifted several high-ranking employees into mid-level positions, and then proclaimed he was addressing the crisis. Alvarez, however, failed to propose building even one new unit of housing. He was addressing the "crisis" as he was interested in defining it, and the media praised his actions. This was not, however, the same crisis with which we were primarily concerned.

The second dilemma inherent in pursuing a public corruption campaign was that we might be compelled to ally with forces that actively oppose public corruption, but that directly benefit from the housing crisis and, therefore, actively oppose efforts to build more low-income housing.

While they oppose the corruption that pilfers their tax money, many wealthy interests directly benefited from the real estate "boom," and the bad public policies that exacerbated it, which we strongly oppose. Walking hand in hand with wealthy interests one day and then facing loggerheads the next could prove a delicate dance, particularly as they try to co-opt us or dominate the public debate so that our issue never sees the light of day.

As such, we resolved that we would use public corruption as leverage to win gains for our anti-gentrification fight, but that none of the progressive forces would exert significant time in that part of the movement.

PUBLIC POLICY.

While corruption was the centerpiece of the media series, the real issue for most activists was the public policy—both stated and unstated—of housing.

At the time, over 41,000 families languished on the housing assistance waiting list, a number that surely would grow were the list reopened to allow more to join. The number of housing units lost to the hands of public corruption was shocking, and yet paled in comparison to the number of units destroyed, left vacant or otherwise made unavailable due to the public policy decisions of elected and housing agency officials.

Ironically, while the media focused on corruption to the complete exclusion of policy, even a cursory examination of the many bizarre policy decisions rendered surely would uncover even more corruption.

More important for us, given the current situation, one could imagine a scenario in which there was no public corruption, but still severe gentrification and a lack of low-income housing due to bad public policy, including decisions to demolish existing, or refrain from building new, low-income housing units.

On balance and for most involved, the public policy aspect of the crisis was more important than the corruption side because it held the potential for the greatest increase in the number of housing units available for low-income people.

The decision was made, then, to coalesce the major housing and anti-gentrification forces in South Florida into this part of the movement to take advantage of this unique opportunity in time and exact concessions from a target who has been, to this point, unwilling to budge on any front.

Demands were developed around the public policy part, creating the foundation for what became the Emergency Housing Coalition. The goal of this coalition was to change the public policy of housing among local governments as a means of addressing the crisis of gentrification and housing.

There remained, then, one other movement area to define and address.

SYSTEMIC ISSUES.

Given the "parts of the movement" framework accepted by the group, a new proposition was forwarded: since it is possible, in theory anyway, for there to be no corruption and due to bad public policy, still face a crisis of gentrification and housing, is it possible for there to be 'good' public policy and still the same crisis?

In other words, is the system that prioritizes profit over people (capitalism), devalues black lives (white supremacy) and discounts the economic and social value of women's work, particularly as the raisers of tomorrow's society (patriarchy), even capable of providing decent and affordable housing for all people?

We say no.

It is entirely possible, we argued, that elected officials could stop stealing and correct public policy, but that the economic and social scale was tilted so sharply towards profit over people, that a disproportionate number of poor black women would still lack decent and humane housing.

While we unified with the objective of building more low-income housing, the scope of poverty reaches beyond the mere number of units of housing available. Other economic and social considerations beyond the narrow confines of local housing policy contribute to, even cause and maintain, the kind of poverty only laid bare by the housing crisis.

The housing crisis, then, is not in and of itself the problem. Rather, the housing crisis is a glaring symptom of a larger, deeper problem rooted in class, race and gender. Those are the Systemic Issues.

The fact is, there are greater economic rewards, and fewer punishments, for running a slum than for providing sufficient amounts of decent housing for low-income people. As important as public policy might be—and it is—no amount of tinkering will override the structural issues which lead directly to profitable slums and the intentional under-building of low-income housing.

Important public policy changes can and must be made in every city facing this crisis. Further, it is the obligation of social justice workers to fight diligently for those changes because they improve the lives of human beings. However, those public policy campaigns cannot mask the real structural and systemic problems contributing to poverty, racism and sexism.

Examples of the systemic nature of many social problems are abundant: feeding or housing the homeless seemingly fails to reduce the overall percentage of homeless people; the shocking number of arrests, incarcerations and long sentences in the U.S. does not reduce the crime rate. It is as if homelessness and crime are integral and necessary parts of this economic and social system. If you house a homeless person or incarcerate a criminal, society just "produces" replacements.

Researching gentrification theories reveals interesting and provocative explanations for this phenomenon and potential mitigators to its devastating impacts. Interestingly enough, few, if any, theories argue that gentrification itself can be stopped, because its cause is so deeply rooted in the cycles of the broader economic system. Even the business community insists gentrification is inevitable and unstoppable because it is the result of nothing less than the market itself at work. The destruction of communities and lives is the market at work.

The idea is powerful, scary and crystal clear: public policy changes alone cannot stop gentrification because gentrification is the market at work, an integral part of the economic system itself. According to the economists themselves, the only way to stop gentrification is to stop the market from working; to change economic systems to one less efficient, perhaps, but more humane.

Perpetual homelessness, street level crime and brutal cycles of gentrification are inevitable parts of the current economic and social systems. The powerful prey on the economically and politically weak, meting out disproportionate suffering among blacks and women. These are systemic issues which can only be addressed as such.

If, then, gentrification, and the "real estate booms" that promote it, are cyclical and integral parts of the economic system, then no amount of public policy reform will solve the problem. The problem must be solved on a systemic or root level.

The root issue at stake: land.

The charge to the movement was now clear: allow the powers and other interests to address the issue of public corruption; the progressive organizations take on the issue of public policy; and the Pan-African forces identify and take on the systemic issues of land control and alternate economic and social models.

It was at this moment—before it was named, prior to the first meeting and even without agreed-upon principles and objectives—that Take Back the Land was born.

Volunteers trained residents to build their own shanties.

Resident Jonathan Baker shows off his home.

To build support and fill a need, a children's activities area was created and stocked.

4. The Black Response

AS THE MOVEMENT PARTS—public corruption, public policy and systemic issues—began to shape up, I moved forward with the research, theory and general organizing of the response to the systemic issues. The research was not limited to potential solutions to systemic issues, as I worked on some public policy ideas as well. I developed theories and plans while anxiously awaiting the call to attend the initial meetings of the public policy area.

Even though the bulk of my time would be devoted to the systemic issues part of the movement, I felt that providing political clarity and pushing the hard political line would help shape the direction of the public policy part while, simultaneously, ensuring some level of coordination between the two.

So, I was more than a little surprised when informed that the initial meeting of the public policy group had already taken place. When the plan was discussed and agreed upon, I was supposed to be included in the meeting. I was not the lead in the public policy part, and each part was to operate under its own relative autonomy, granted the power to make strategic decisions without being second-guessed about every little thing. Yet still, I could not help but to feel slighted.

I did receive an e-mail, along with others, recapping the initial meeting. I replied with suggestions on language and positions, and then expressed dismay at my exclusion from the meeting and demanded, from my own allies, that I be included in the next meeting of the group I was told I was a part of. The response was that everyone realized I should have been there at the meeting and would definitely be invited to the next.

A few days later, several sources informed me that the follow-up meeting to the Emergency Housing Coalition was scheduled. Again I was not invited, nor were several other prominent blacks active in the political and housing scene, such as Leroy Jones, who led the charge against the original HOPE VI proposal at Scott-Carver and Marleine Bastien, the most prominent Haitian activist in Florida, who explicitly expressed interest in the group. The lack of invitation seemed more than mere oversight.

THE MYTH OF COALITION

The lessons we learn over and again, most of the time the hard way, is that coalitions are a tricky maneuver, and it is difficult for the black community to enter into coalitions, even with those whom we like or agree with politically, from positions of political or economic weakness.

Even if we have much to contribute, from a position of weakness we have little leverage from which to force our demands and other, more powerful coalition members will run us over. Oftentimes, the most powerful leverage point we have is to undermine or destroy the coalition itself, a move that hurts the community as much as it hurts the powerhouses of the coalition.

This is not an argument against coalitions or partnerships, as they are extremely useful in expanding capacity and demonstrating broad support for correct political positions and campaigns. Rather, it is recognition that if and when we join other coalitions, we are helping their agenda, not necessarily our own. To be clear, there is nothing wrong with helping to advance an agenda that is not your own when you support that agenda. In this instance, however, the agenda should have been led by the black community and our unique interests should have been front and center, not lost in the watered-down final agreement.

In the end, the Emergency Housing Coalition did excellent work under difficult circumstances. It pushed a generally progressive agenda, won some victories, made some tactical errors and lost some battles. The Coalition did not, however, represent the views and leadership of the black community. The exclusion of critical elements of progressive Black leadership, as well as several subsequent missteps, was troubling in many respects.

Whatever the missteps, the experience made clear that the black community had a lot of development to do in order to build enough internal power to start our own coalitions, deciding who to and who not to invite—or, at the very least, so that others could not advance coalitions impacting our community without us.

Toward those ends, it was clear that the systemic issues part of this movement must be an all African formation in order to address the systemic issues associated with land and gentrification, the current state of the progressive movement, and the internal development and capacity of the black community.

Consequently, it was important to assemble a core group of individuals who were dedicated to the cause of African Liberation, even if they, individually, lacked some of the skill sets associated with professional organizers. Of course, this category includes me, as I continue to develop my own skills. Most importantly, in the end, the effort would serve to expand the skill set and collective capacity of the black community.

I invited a small group of activists, each of whom has demonstrated their commitment to the advancement of our community, to attend the initial meeting of what we then called the Black Response to the Housing Crisis, which evolved into Take Back the Land.

The truth is that I did not get along with every single person invited. Ironically, I had a very stand-offish relationship with General Rashid, President of Brothers of the Same Mind and stalwart of N'COBRA (National Coalition of Blacks for Reparations in America) and the PGRNA (Provisional Government of the Republic of New Afrika), but soon, his steady hand was indispensable to our theory and decision making process.

In addition to the initial group of invitees, there were two others I sought out for the Black Response: Amanda Seaton and Poncho, two extremely bright and dedicated sistas. I honestly believed that with the two of them at the core, we could build a movement that would impact land and housing struggles in South Florida.

Unfortunately for us, Amanda was employed elsewhere. We only ran into each other occasionally, but whenever she spoke of her work, one could feel her passion and witness her devotion. Amanda conjures images of a hippie, laid back and cool, interested in a broad range of issues, bringing a unique perspective to discussions about class and race. As such, I felt it was difficult for her to fit into any one political setting and, consequently, her skills would always be underutilized. What was clear was that she belonged in the leadership of an organization somewhere. We had not spoken in a while, but after asking around, I discovered she was working, so I moved on to other options.

Poncho and I met while working together on AmBush, a campaign to ensure George W. Bush would not be re-elected, or re-selected, president. She was very clear on her political line and impressively uncompromising in its application. What I remembered most, however, was her razor-sharp wit. Poncho had a snappy line for every possible occasion, and most of them were political. She was funny, smart and great to be around. Poncho was available, but informed me that she was not ready to just jump into some hare-brained scheme. She had things to do and places to go, but wanted to remain in the loop, so I called her regularly with updates and encouraged her, over and over again, to join the Black Response.

The Black Response group met religiously every Saturday at Marleine Bastien's FANM offices, which she graciously made available. The configuration of the group changed somewhat from week to week, but the core included myself, Jewel Parham, General Rashid and Patty Macias.

On occasion, Kobina Bantushango, organizer for the International Peoples' Democratic Uhuru Movement, popularly known as InPDUM or Uhuru, showed up and contributed greatly. Kobina was in Miami organizing around the notorious Liberty City 7 case, in which seven black men were indicted on trumped-up terrorism charges.

The initial task of the group was to establish principles (what we believed) and objectives (our political goals) upon which we were organized. A clear framework ensured we all agreed on what we were doing and why we were doing it. General Rashid's years of experience were invaluable in this context, as he forced us to discuss, in detail, ideas and positions that we only thought we understood, such as our relationship to elected officials, to each other, to allies, to other coalitions working on the issue and to the community as a whole.

The end result was not that we always agreed, but that we were clear on what we agreed about and equally as clear on what we disagreed about.

Clearly understanding each other's positions and views is critical to building any coalition. Glossing over differences might be harmless when the campaign around which the coalition is built consists of one simple step. In virtually any other scenario, however, glossing over differences in order to build "unity" in the short term will result in chaos in the long term.

The primary benefit to the exhaustive, and oft-times frustrating, process of achieving mutual clarity is not agreement, it is understanding precisely where each party stands on the relevant points and issues. Only this understanding determines whether the coalition is a viable one.

This understanding also prevents the folly, and subsequent disappointment, that occurs when coalescing parties assume that because all agree on point A and point B, it necessarily follows that all agree on point C.

Oftentimes, for the sake of "unity," critical, and often insurmountable, differences are ignored or simply glossed over. However, those differences exist whether or not they are discussed. And as uncomfortable as it might be to discuss them before the campaign gets going, imagine the difficulty in discussing them in the heat of a high-stakes campaign, during which any fallout entails bad implications.

So, we spent countless afternoon hours discussing the finer points of land struggle, history and current events in South Florida. Everyone had an opportunity to state their opinions and we challenged each other, not for the sake of arguing or in bad faith, but as a part of the process of understanding each other and building unity.

We agreed that our core interest was not limited to the issue of gentrification, but encompassed the broader concept of land struggle. We agreed that an all-African group must provide political leadership for the solution to the problems in the African (black) community, but that we were free to work with non-black groups and individuals, provided they were willing to operate under black leadership. And we agreed to focus our attention on low-income black people, not the black middle class. Once we agreed on a certain number of facts and interpretations, it was time to move towards developing our program.

The guiding assumption was that there is little point in seeking help from the government, as the government is largely responsible for this mess in the first place. If they had not responded to the years of begging, pleading and demanding, it was not because they were unaware of the problems or unable to address them—it was because they did not want to.

As such, our program would not be fashioned around what we believed we could procure from this elected official or elicit from that bureaucrat, it would be built around what we could do for ourselves. Our model, then, was not dependent upon the power of elected officials, but rooted in the power of our community.

PLANNING A TAKEOVER

Our initial plan was to take over—we called it "liberating"—vacant units of public housing. The units were vacant, belonged to the people and represented the failures of government in providing adequate housing. We talked about locations, including the possibility of taking over an entire vacant building at the Scott-Carver projects, which had been largely demolished at the hands of the HOPE VI program and the focal point of the media stories which ignited the recent furor.

The idea was to find families on the housing wait list and pair them up with vacant public housing units compatible with their needs. We would rehab the units, then move the family in and mobilize community support around the family's right to stay.

There were two move-in lists: public and private. The list name did not refer to the ownership of the units, but to the manner in which the families would be moved. Some would be moved in a very public way, with full media and a public defense of their right to remain. Others would be moved in privately, without a word, a surreptitious occupation.

The two types of moves represented two different, and almost mutually exclusive, political objectives: the first was to expose contradictions in the system and the second was to provide housing.

While a "public" take over, with plenty of media and a community mobilization, would expose the contradictions of the system, the likelihood of arrests meant the action would not provide long-term housing for those in need. Conversely, surreptitious move-ins, on the down-low, sneaking families into housing under the cover of night, might provide housing, but would not raise the issue for public discourse, exposing the failures of the system—a critical component addressing the issue on the systemic level. So, two dispositions of the same act were required in order to meet the broad nature of our objectives.

This pairing out of tactics demonstrated another valuable lesson—establish clear political objectives. The appropriate action is entirely dependent upon the political objective. It is tempting to start with a great tactic and plan backwards to the objective, but a tactic is nothing more, or less, than a means of achieving an objective. Therefore, occupying a building is only a great action if that action advances pre-existing political objectives. If it does not, then it is not a great action. Can't decide between two or more seemingly great actions? Clarify the objective and the appropriate action will probably make itself known.

In any event, liberating housing units advanced the objective of addressing the crisis on a systemic level. We were not asking the powers to move people in, we were taking power and moving people in ourselves. This was a significant shift in the approach to problems in our community, a shift from which many of us are now reluctant to return.

DESPERATE TIMES, DESPERATE MEASURES

Two families lined up to move in before our plans were finalized. We were contacted by a lady who heard about us through a friend of a friend who attended a meeting. She recently lost her job while recovering from cancer treatments. She and her two children were about to be evicted from their slum apartment and she was in the 31,000s of the housing assistance wait list.

As we talked she expressed her apprehension, both at her own situation and at the potential solution. But she was so desperate, she was willing to try almost anything.

Perhaps it was the fact that she was a desperate woman in a desperate situation, but I felt obliged to not just be honest, but to be explicit with her about the risks for arrest and the potential for a media circus. I told her we would have lawyers and the media attention might even get her a place from a sympathetic observer or a municipal government trying to quell a growing firestorm.

I also told her that she could get arrested, she would be in the news and it would be a hectic and chaotic scene, one that could be scary and difficult to deal with, particularly for the children. I told her this was a historic moment, and that the only reason she can work and move about freely today is because of the sacrifices made by our elders and ancestors in days past. I told her the action would help countless people get housing and that she was brave for even considering participation.

It's important to be perfectly honest with the people at all times, making clear the risks, and trusting them to make informed decisions about their level of participation. The easy route would be to minimize the risks or pep-talk her into doing something that she was not ready to do, a tempting option given the fact that the issue at hand was much bigger than her and her family. Furthermore, the idea of the county, on the heels of a massive scandal, coming in on television to evict a cancer survivor and her children—who occupy number 31,000 on the wait list—from perfectly good housing that had remained vacant for two years, was almost irresistible.

Almost.

She thanked me for my honesty and informed me of her heart condition. She explained that due to a previous run-in with police, to this day when a cop drives behind her, her heart jumps into her throat. If they came in yelling and screaming, she feared she might literally have a heart attack in front of everyone. She was desperate, but had to think about this one. I gave her the numbers of a few agencies, thanked her for being so brave, apologized for things being so hard for her family, and hung up the phone. She never called back and I never forced the issue. I often wonder where she is today.

Given how far along we were in our planning process—not very far— and the kinds of responses we had already received, we were confident in our plan and our chances for success.

THE POTTINGER SETTLEMENT

With our framing of land and basic game plan of taking over public housing under development, I researched related political movements, historic and contemporary, and mulled practical considerations such as squatters' rights and the like, and came across a famous Miami legal case, the Pottinger Settlement. I became aware of the Pottinger lawsuit when it was settled, with great fanfare, in 1996. I was not familiar with the details, just that it was a landmark settlement strengthening the rights of one of society's most vulnerable groups, the homeless, and was used as a model in many parts of the country.

I also remembered the case because I met the suit's lead attorney, Benji Waxman, through John De Leon, then president of the Miami Chapter of the ACLU, of which Benji and I are also members. John essentially bridged the gap between the Greater Miami ACLU and the black community in the late 1990s with his tireless visits to our neighborhoods and his ardent support for our struggle against police brutality and other injustices. When John left Miami to help structure the public defender system in Columbia, Lida Rodriguez-Taseff picked up right where he left off. Not that it doesn't have any improvements to make, but John and Lida are the primary reasons why the Miami Chapter of the ACLU is one of the best as it relates to its work in the black community.

As to Pottinger, In the late 1980s, the City of Miami police routinely arrested homeless people and jailed them for little or no cause. In many instances, the cops would steal the meager belongings of the homeless, or even pile up the belongings and set them aflame. These types of police assaults increased as major events, such as the Super Bowl, came to town, as the powers-that-be had an interest concealing the homeless population. The ACLU sued, Benji argued, and the city settled.

In the settlement, the City of Miami begrudgingly and reluctantly, but legally, concedes that being homeless is not against the law. Therefore, anyone who is homeless and on government property, while there are no other alternatives—i.e. no available beds in a local homeless shelter—cannot be arrested for engaging in "life sustaining conduct." Such conduct includes bathing, changing, socializing, eating, sleeping, making fires to cook, "responding to calls of nature," and erecting "temporary shelters" to protect oneself from the elements, among other acts. Conduct such as using drugs, stealing, vandalizing, etc., are of course, not protected by Pottinger. Also, if there were beds available in local shelters, the police could compel the homeless person to check into the shelter or face jail. When there are no beds in the shelter, however, Pottinger was on.

The light bulbs were flashing. If one homeless person could engage in "life sustaining conduct," could two do so together? Or five? Or fifty?

Benji and I batted around thoughts, ideas and scenarios, and he answered a good number of questions, but wanted to review the original documents again and bring in another great movement attorney, Ray Taseff, into the discussion. When we next spoke, they both seemed to believe that if a group of homeless people built "temporary structures" on public land in Miami, the community was technically protected by Pottinger.

However, Ray and Benji warned that while the idea appeared protected in theory, the city clearly did not anticipate this type of application of the law and would likely respond with arrests, or worse. And even though the Pottinger Settlement was law, the lawyers could not predict how the arrests would play out because the law was largely untested in court.

More to the point, the state will not sit idly by while we take what they consider to be their land. So, the lawyers suggested that after we arrive on the land and the police show up, we make our point and then avoid arrest. If we did get arrested, it is not all that clear how the cases would shake out, because even though the settlement seems clear, one never knows how certain judges rule in conservative districts, such as the one in which we would face trial.

While all of this was great legal advice, and we appreciated the honest and professional legal analysis, the interests of the lawyers to keep us out of jail at any cost conflicted with the interests of the movement to advance our program, which might require us to face arrest. Ray, as always, agreed to represent us if we were arrested and Benji agreed to help. Our job was to advance the movement; their job was to get us cleared of all charges. With a superstar legal team in place, we were ready for just about any action and any consequence.

BLACK POLITICAL LEADERSHIP

Back in the Black Response meetings, our strategy shifted according to the new information: since one of our objectives was to actually provide housing for people, not just expose contradictions or protest, the legal protections offered by Pottinger were attractive. We still wanted to take over vacant public and privately owned units, but enjoyed limited legal protections. Taking over land, under the auspices of Pottinger, gave full legal protection to our actions while detracting nothing. The only difference of significance is that our base population would shift from the under-housed homeless population to the street-homeless population.

A revised plan emerged: take over a piece of public land and take arrests, if necessary. Once we established the legitimacy of Pottinger in court, we would stretch its very limits by taking over public housing, taking arrests there, and arguing there is no fundamental difference between vacant public land and vacant public housing, and that the homeless had the same rights to both.

We were all excited about the idea of taking over land, particularly General Rashid, who had spent a lifetime discussing the concept inside of the PGRNA. If we survived the arrests, we would build a shantytown where the homeless could live in dignity, even if not in luxury, for free. We would feed and politicize them through political education sessions.

Our principles and objectives were set, our two-step plan of action was in place and the Black Response was ready to move forward.

With our action plan solid, I approached Poncho to make one more pitch for her participation. We reviewed the plan and she was sold. She was not only willing to participate, but she wanted to participate on a high level and take the lead in organizing certain aspects of the concept.

A few days later, I discovered that Amanda left her job. I immediately contacted her, we met up and I made the pitch. She asked a lot of questions and generally seemed skeptical of our capacity to pull off such an ambitious project. She was very coy about her willingness to participate, and downright standoffish about playing any type of leadership role. Amanda later told me she thought the idea was crazy and doomed to failure. Naturally, she signed up.

At this point, we were clear about our objectives and plans, but there remained a gap between what we wanted to do and our ability to actually do it. Collectively, particularly with the addition of Poncho and Amanda, we had a broad skill set, but it was not broad or deep enough to build a city, which is essentially the task with which we charged ourselves. We had to construct living spaces, bathroom facilities and food preparation areas, and it was not clear that we could do that on our own.

As part of our weekly conversations, we regularly discussed theories behind coalition building and strategic partnerships. We were clear that coalitions were difficult, but also useful when properly structured and executed.

What we needed was a strategic partnership with allies able to fill in the gaps left by our skill set. However, the arrangement would only work if the partners were overtly and openly willing to operate under black political leadership.

In other words, we would partner with other groups or individuals who shared our general vision for Liberty City and the shantytown. But the partnership would not be one where everyone is in the room together voting on all the same things with the same amount of power.

The partners would be given their task, and the space to complete the task, but would operate explicitly under the black political leadership of the core formed by the Black Response. We would make the broader political decisions and the partners would be empowered to make all the decisions necessary to fully achieve their objectives.

THE CRUNCHY KIDS

During the 2003 Free Trade Area of the Americas (FTAA) Ministerial, protests against so-called "free trade" erupted in Miami as they did elsewhere in the world over the same subject. As part of the process of planning and participating in the protests—I worked for the Miami Workers Center and helped organize the Root Cause 34-mile march—I had the pleasure and honor of working with several anarchist groups, including a loosely associated but highly dedicated group of young people, Lake Worth Global Justice. We called them the Lake Worth Kids. Others called them Granola or the Crunchy Kids.

During the planning and the protests themselves, the Kids showed incredible resourcefulness in their efforts not to waste or spend too much money, and in their love for the cause and each other. I watched in awe as Panagioti, Rebecca, Waffle, Lynne, Cara and many others put their bodies and freedom on the line for what they believed. They were great to work with.

I kept in touch with Panagioti and Waffle and saw Rebecca, who is not from Lake Worth, on occasion, and was looking for the next opportunity for us to work together. As I sketched out what constructing a small city might entail, I knew that time had arrived.

Once the Black Response agreed on the ground rules of the strategic partnership, we were able to get several Kids in the same room at the same time to pitch the idea.

I talked about the housing crisis and how parts of the movement were addressing corruption and public policy, and how the Black Response was to address the underlying structural issues associated with the crisis. We discussed collective community relationships to land, and we talked about building an urban shantytown.

The Kids loved the concept and committed to spreading the word through their informal network and identifying dates when large numbers of them could travel from Lake Worth, or other parts of the country, and stay for a week or more to build.

We met twice more to discuss details and plan. Most importantly, the Kids fully agreed to work under the black political leadership we provided. The strategic partnership provides a model for a specific kind of coalition that can, and should, be duplicated. In any event, with the final piece of the puzzle solved, we were ready to build ourselves a shantytown.

Mr. Roosevelt, Fred Young and Lanish.

John Cata.

Serge Rameau and Brion Jones.

5. Land and Gentrifcation

THE UMOJA VILLAGE SHANTYTOWN received its share of press, mostly focused on the embarrassment it caused to Miami-Dade County and the City of Miami. Attention was also appropriately lavished on the nexus between gentrification, the housing crisis, the role of the government in manufacturing that crisis and the number of people homeless—both street and under-housed—in South Florida.

While all of that is well and good, such coverage expended a disproportionate amount of attention on the tip of the iceberg visible above the water, and not nearly enough attention on the humongous glacier lurking below the surface. The tendency is understandable, as the current events type of news generally covers what is happening, leaving the more significant questions, such as "why is this happening" to other genres, such as history and academia. I will refrain from calculating the impact of conflicts of interest on the corporate media.

News coverage of the 'what' is sufficient for most, but anyone studying, much less engaged in, liberation struggles must search deeper and come to understand the 'why.' Only by struggling with the 'why' can we understand the significance and context of the 'what,' and determine appropriate responses or courses of action.

SURFACE VS. ROOT ISSUES

In order to properly analyze any social dilemma or contradiction, it is critical to distinguish between the surface issues at play and the root issues at stake.

Surface issues are those that directly and tangibly confront the society and its members, those issues on the surface, to the forefront and in our face. Surface issues often grab attention, mobilize people and reveal the existence and importance of a deeper problem.

The surface issue, however compelling, is only the manifestation or symptom of the deeper, more significant problem, the fundamental or root issue. Conversely, the root issue is the cause of the surface issue.

This distinction is important to make, because no matter how vigorously one attacks a symptom, the only way to solve a problem is by resolving its cause, not its symptom. This is not to say that surface issues, or symptoms, should be ignored, but rather that we should understand that addressing the symptom is no substitute for addressing the root cause.

For example, a dinner party patron who develops a runny nose would do well to acquire napkins and wipe as often as necessary. At the same time, it must be understood that while the runny nose is problematic, it is not the actual problem, but rather the untimely symptom of a deeper problem and sickness. While our patron cannot be expected to enjoy the soirée by ignoring the constant nasal drip, it must be clear that the napkin is not curing the sickness, it is merely masking its symptoms from the other dinner guests.

If the root cause of the problem is never addressed, one could, conceivably, spend their entire life wiping, dabbing, blowing and otherwise dealing with a symptom, a symptom that would disappear on its own if only the underlying sickness, the root issue, were addressed.

The perils of failing to distinguish between a symptom and the problem that causes the symptom—the surface issue vs. the root issue—is not limited to those with active social calendars: it continues to confuse and confound liberation and social justice movements. The failure to understand the difference between surface and root issues will convince us we are making progress when we are making none; that we are moving forward when we are running around in circles; and that we have solved a problem, when in fact we are only altering the manifestation of that problem.

Consequently, the crisis of gentrification and low-income housing mandates a thorough examination and analysis of the surface and root issues at stake.

As bad as it is, this crisis, at least as it relates to the black community, is a surface issue, a mere symptom of a deeper problem. The crisis touches our lives as we see and feel the impact of law, government expenditures and the mobilization of private capital. Gentrification forces us out of our communities and the lack of low-income housing offers us few options. And yet, gentrification is clearly a surface, not root, issue.

This is no attempt to minimize the importance of gentrification as an economic phenomenon and social issue. Quite to the contrary, gentrification, and our response to it, will likely emerge as a defining issue of this generation. Gentrification destroys homes, separates families and guts historically black communities to make room for whites looking for shorter commutes to work and the arts.

In many ways, gentrification in the 2000s is the functional equivalent of segregation in the 1950s and 60s. Social movements were built around fighting segregation, as students and other sectors of society risked life and limb to fight for its demise. And yet, a proper analysis of history and struggle affirms that segregation was and remains a surface issue, not a root issue.

Because the surface issue of segregation was elevated, in the minds of many, to the status of root issue, it was presumed that the end of segregation, as a set of laws, would end the problem of inequality, codified by those laws.

More than fifty years after the legal walls of segregation began to crumble, the races in the U.S. are still largely separated, if not outright segregated. Most blacks live in overwhelmingly black communities and most whites live in overwhelmingly white communities. Thanks to the defeat of legal segregation—a noble cause that was right to fight—blacks can now sit next to whites in restaurants, on the bus and even in the stall of the public bathroom, before each returns to their respective racially separate neighborhoods and houses of worship. Poverty and unemployment in the black community remains disproportionate to that suffered by whites and discrimination remains rampant, even if technically illegal.

Of course the powers-that-be, particularly through the use of the media, cultural outlets and the educational system, had an interest in advancing the notion that a root issue had been resolved and, therefore, the society was just, and the need for struggle ended.

As a result, many in the social justice movement were thoroughly confused and confounded by how segregation was defeated, but racism and inequality persisted. If segregation were in fact a root issue, or a cause, then the elimination of the Jim Crow laws would end the problems of racism and inequality.

Racism and inequality did not end with the fall of Jim Crow because segregation was not the cause of racism and inequality, it was the symptom. Jim Crow laws were the manifestation of the hate whites bore against blacks and the specific rules of White Supremacy and privilege. But the root issue never was eating in a specific restaurant or drinking water from a particular fountain.

The root issue was not segregation, it was White Supremacy and power. Consequently, fifty years after the fall of legal segregation, widespread de-facto segregation persists, the black community faces many of the same challenges it did then, and whites continue to derive privilege from their whiteness.

Just as the best way to stop a runny nose is not to wipe, but to cure the sickness that causes it, the best way to stop segregation is not to end the laws, but to end the ideology that spurred its existence in the first place.

As an aside, people differ on what qualifies as a root issue for them. While most fought segregation as a means of addressing the root issue of discrimination and inequality, some people fought segregation because they wanted to live next to white people or eat in fancy restaurants.

U.S. Secretary of State Condoleezza Rice has told of how, in segregated Alabama, white store owners allowed her mother to shop at their businesses, albeit after hours, even while excluding the general black population. To Rice's family, the root issue was literally segregation—their right to buy from racist store owners with access to cute outfits. And to people like Rice, the struggle is over, as she can now shop, dine and live where she wants. For others, however, there are deeper principles at stake, and we continue to fight until those principles are realized.

The same model and pattern applies to the fight against gentrification. Under segregation, the larger white community ordered blacks to live in this area, and we were compelled to comply. At the end of legal segregation, most stayed in the black community while others thought they were leaving, but ultimately succeeded only in convincing white people to move out of their neighborhood to make room for a new black community.

Today, under gentrification, some in the white community want to move back into historically black communities, forcing blacks to vacate and make room for them, and we are again compelled to comply.

What is the objective difference, in the context of our human rights and political power, between the 1950s and the early 2000s? In both instances, rich whites make money off of the backs of poor blacks; the government is used to enforce the geopolitical objectives of the larger white community, particularly the wealthier whites who covet the inexpensive and strategically situated black neighborhood; and black families have little real power to determine, on their own, where they will live. In segregation, we were forced into one area and in gentrification, we are forced out of one area. What is the objective difference between the 1950s and today?

We repeat history because during the civil rights movement, we fought the symptom of the problem, not the actual problem. Consequently, just like the party patron who wipes one runny nostril only to get that drippy feeling from the other, our failure to deal with the root issues—not the segregation laws, but the reason why those laws were enacted in the first place— is coming back to haunt us.

The root issue then was not segregation and the root issue now is not gentrification. The root issue is land.

Not just land in the physical sense of the word, although that is included, but land in the political sense of the word, meaning power and control over land. Land is an essential element of liberation, an absolute prerequisite. The lack of power and control over land condemns the majority of African (black) people in America to an endless cycle of moving from one undesirable lot to the next, at the behest and for the benefit of the rich.

This reality demonstrates how differentiating between surface and root issues brings clarity to our analysis and enables us to gauge progress, or the lack thereof.

Those who believe that segregation itself was root or fundamental, argue forcefully that the struggle is, for all intents and purposes, over. However, those who understand land as root and segregation as symptomatic, recognize just how little progress has been made. The same segments of society which confined us to one geographical area then are able to, with relative ease, force us off of those same geographical areas 50 years later. They are able to do so precisely because, in relation to control over land, the black community has no more power today than we had prior to the civil rights movement.

It is easy to see that while much movement has occurred, little tangible progress has been made in dealing with the root issue of power and control over land.

To be thorough and fair, it is often argued that there are really two root causes at stake here, both land and racism—or White Supremacy—and that ending the root issue of White Supremacy would have also ended segregation. While that might be true, the reality is that ending White Supremacy and hate in someone else is neither easy nor a substitute for building power for oneself. Even if we were willing and able to devote our entire existence and all our resources towards the task of teaching whites to hate us less, after the successful completion of the mission, we would still have before us the task of building power and control over land. Therefore, the issue of land—more specifically, power and collective control over land—is root and primary.

Those who benefit from our misery, of course, would rather that we only address the surface issues and then give up the struggle after making progress on that front. Our mission and objectives must be more substantial, however. Sickness cannot be cured by wiping a runny nose and liberation cannot be achieved by setting our sights on superficial changes that do not address the root causes of exploitation and oppression.

For these reasons and others, it is clear that in order to address the crisis of gentrification and low-income housing in a real way, our responses must be rooted in land-based solutions.

The work of Take Back the Land is not fundamentally about the homeless, or even gentrification; it is fundamentally about the collective control over land.

Umoja often provided activities
for neighborhood children.

Tough guys playing football on the land.

DJ Scribe entertains the Village and friends.

6. October 23, 2006

THE LEADERSHIP TEAM CAREFULLY crafted political unity, the Lake Worth Kids prepared to build a city and the legal team was in place and ready to defend us. We were ready to Take Back the Land.

Because of the legal implications involved, a certain number of security precautions were required. As such, a choice few were privy to both the action's date and location.

The Lake Worth Kids were coming for a week to help set up the shantytown, so they had to know the dates. In early October, I took a handful of them to look at approximately twenty potential sites in Overtown, Little Haiti and Liberty City. In Overtown, we looked at the Sawyers Walk lot, which was slated for a gentrification project by the Michigan based Crosswinds corporation, making the site ideal in a number of respects. We also looked at the vacant lot next to the office of Power U, potentially providing us with a friendly neighbor, ideal for emergency electricity and water.

The Kids explained the pros and cons of each site we visited, and I listened intently to become qualified to make the final decision.

Our legal team knew the action would take place in late October, but not much else. As the date approached, they were made aware that it would take place in Liberty City, so that they generally knew where to head if and when the arrests started.

In the end, I selected a vacant lot on the corner of 62nd Street and NW 17th Avenue in Liberty City. That lot formerly housed the Martin Luther King Apartments, a three-story green building that featured a curved corner, noticeable as one traveled west on 62nd Street, with the curve tempting one around to 17th Avenue.

In 1997, residents of the complex had contacted Leroy Jones, activist extraordinaire and founder of Brothers of the Same Mind, to complain about living conditions there. Because the property was owned by a politically-connected slumlord, the city had refused to compel the owner to make necessary repairs. Months after Leroy complained to the city to no avail, a child had slipped through the loose third-floor balcony railings—which had been one of the complaints—and was injured in the fall. Both the medics and the media had arrived on the scene.

Left with no option, the city had finally inspected the building and was forced to condemn each and every unit. The residents were forced out and, with just twenty-four hours notice, had to come up with first, last and a security deposit, as well as find a place willing to take them.

The following year, the City of Miami punished the slumlord by purchasing the building for $900,000. This was in 1998, prior to the housing boom, and therefore way overpriced, particularly for what amounted to a useless slab of concrete. The city then demolished the building and repeated the process with several other buildings on 61st and 60th Streets, between 17th and 12th Avenues.

Leroy and I complained harshly to then Commissioner Art Teele—including one incident when I was "asked" to leave his State of the District address in the Edison Middle School auditorium—until the city relented, signing contracts with each of the 482 families dislocated by the purchasing and demolition spree. Each family was contractually assured the right to return to the new units built by the city. Needless to say, after millions of dollars, not one of the units has been built, but the area has suffered a reduction in low-income housing and a depletion of our population.

On the selected land, the smaller back portion of the lot, totaling less than 7,000 square feet, was owned by Miami-Dade County, the target of the "House of Lies" media series. This location allowed us to stick it simultaneously to the city and county.

BUILDING SUPPORT

As the takeover date neared, it was important to build support in the community for our action, but without blowing our cover. The outreach process started more than a month prior as we visited the near-by Liberty Square public housing projects, also known as the "Pork and Beans." The Beans are a hot bed of political activity, in no small part due to the ongoing work of the Miami Workers Center and the organization they created, Low Income Families Fighting Together (LIFFT).

We talked to the residents about the crisis of housing and gentrification, inviting them and the Liberty Square Tenants' Council to our meeting at the community center.

By chance, the County Commission set their own public hearing on the housing scandal for the same date. This was a real test of our resolve, as the County meeting was high profile and virtually everyone working on the issue would be there, including most of the Tenant Council board. It seemed like the only ones who would not be at the Commission meeting were those not aware of it or those so disgusted by the situation, that they wanted nothing to do with housing meetings. Neither option seemed to leave us with good attendance.

However, due to the "parts of the movement" framework, and our own internal conclusions that the problems of gentrification cannot be solved by making requests at the feet of the elected officials largely responsible for the crisis in the first place, we decided that our actions would be based on the internal will and capacity of our community, not the largesse of government officials. Therefore, demanding and begging elected officials was not on our agenda.

We stuck to our orientation and skipped the big show in order to move forward with our meeting and our own agenda. Approximately twenty residents, including one Tenants' Council representative, showed to discuss taking control of our community. The meeting was a success.

After a spirited discussion, we dropped the logical conclusion: the only way to address this crisis is to take adversarial control over land in our community. The residents hesitated. They liked the idea, but wanted more time to think about it. While they supported the idea, each resident expressed concern about their own participation, including concerns about reprisals from the County government who served as their landlord.

Amanda, Poncho and other volunteers went door-to-door talking to neighbors about the housing crisis and how we must "Take Back the

Land" in our community in order to solve our own problems. People were into the talk, but it was difficult to make the concept concrete without revealing details that compromised our security concerns. Surely some we spoke to were tired of hearing the rhetoric and just assumed we were trash talkers coming to push our line.

Residents of the privately-owned slums were generally more militant than those living in public housing. In the apartment complex next to the land that would become Umoja, our future neighbors were distraught at the housing crisis and fed up with government promises and inaction. Several residents invited me to experience the dilapidated conditions under which they lived and it was nothing short of criminal, at least in the moral sense of the term. They were genuinely excited when we talked about taking over land, but I'm not certain they always understood the implications therein. I took a chance and discussed the specifics of the plan with several neighbors, confiding that we would build a shantytown on the adjacent lot, without revealing dates. The excitement and support was palpable.

In addition to informing the neighbors, I started informing allied organizations and individuals about the action as well, again, without revealing compromising information. It was surprisingly difficult to reach all of those I wanted to inform, as schedules conflicted and some did not realize the importance of what I wanted to reveal. Tragically, the poor communication later caused friction.

SECURITY CONSIDERATIONS

The most difficult aspect of the security, as well as ethical, considerations was my inability to discuss the details of the action with my partner, Bernadette. We are extremely close, but I was basically starting a new organization, and Bernadette was a member of Power U, an organization already engaged in anti-gentrification work in Miami. As such, we were ethical about conflicts of interests and wanted to avoid creating the appearance that she was simultaneously working in two organizations.

She understood the concept and intent from early on, and knew about the Saturday meetings, but we deliberately refrained from discussing details. Conversely, she told me nothing of internal wranglings of the Emergency Housing Coalition, of which Power U was a member and Take Back the Land was not.

At times, the situation was a bit bizarre, as we both talked on the phone simultaneously, about the same things, but to different people and then did not continue the conversation with each other.

It was difficult being denied her counsel and advice on important issues of direction and strategy, and I developed some level of resentment towards the arrangement. At the same time, we are both extremely respectful of each other's work and responsibilities and were not willing to put those at risk.

As the takeover date approached, I first informed Denise Perry, the executive director of Power U, even before informing Bernadette. When we finally discussed the details, Bernadette was shocked at how far the planning had advanced and we were shocked that one of us was working on something in which the other was not intimately involved.

SUPPORT SERVICES

Understanding that our target homeless population faces acute social service needs, we tried to corral some services in advance of the action. The idea was to bring in social services from the very beginning to help our residents, but that failed for at least two reasons.

First, even before the action, people could sense there was, or would be, some level of animosity between the organizers and local governments. This was problematic because the social service organizations receive their funding from these same governments and were, therefore, more responsive to their funding source than either to us or, frankly, their clients.

Second, I tried to arrange services for an action which, due to security concerns, I was precluded from describing in concept, date or location. Here is a sample conversation:

Me: Hi. We are organizing an action that will bring homeless people together and we want you to provide services. Can you help?
Service Provider: Sure. So, you are organizing a fair?
Me: No, not really a fair.
S.P.: So, you are providing meals on wheels?
Me: Well, we will provide meals, but not on wheels.
S.P.: What is it exactly you are doing?
Me: Um, well, we are helping the homeless, and will be gathering them in one spot, but I can't really tell you more than that.
S.P.: OK... Where you will be gathering them?

Me: Um. I can't really tell you.

S.P.: Alright. When will this be happening?

Me: Um. I, um, I can't really say.

S.P.: (complete and utter silence).

Me: Ok, thanks for your help, I'll just call back later.

It would have been funnier at the time were it not so embarrassing. In any event, it turns out that social service agencies are reluctant to help your action if you are not willing to tell them what you are doing, when you are doing it or where it will be done.

Undeterred, we finalized our plans and got ready for the big day.

OCTOBER 23, 2006

On the morning of October 23, 2006, the black leadership and our supporters gathered at a Liberty City warehouse and packed food, tents, pots, pans, blankets and other items required to build a small city and loaded them onto a hitch trailer. Because not everyone knew the final location, even moments before the action itself, I led the way to the land.

At 3:00PM, roughly twenty-five people arrived onto the vacant lot on the corner of 62nd Street and NW 17th Avenue and divided up into teams. Some picked up trash—eight bags full; the City of Miami owes us!—while others set up tents, and a small crew set up food stations. Of the twenty-five, about five were homeless and just over half were white. It was a scene.

The neighbors came out to the fence and the balcony to watch the spectacle. Suddenly, the relationship between the conversations we have been engaged in over the past week and this action made complete sense. We are taking over the land.

As we arrived, an e-mail blast was sent to our supporters detailing the action. Within 15 minutes my cell phone was blowing up and people started showing up on the land. Some showed up clapping and cheering while others arrived visibly angry, pacing to and fro, engaged in heated condemnation of what was happening on this piece of land in Liberty City. More significantly, the cops showed up ready to make arrests.

The first police car was not even at a full stop when the doors swung open and two jumped out screaming. "Stop right there!" Major Brown is in charge at the Model City police station, just a few blocks down the street, and he was irate.

Poncho had been given the task of talking with the police, but Brown was not trying to hear any of it. She had a handout explaining Pottinger, but he refused to take it and ordered us off the land. We tried to explain our rights, but he just called for backup. As we waited for backup to arrive I walked up to Brown, convinced him to accept a copy of Pottinger, and told him he should read it before arresting us. He angrily shooed me away, so I backed off and our crew talked about who would take arrests and how; it was decided I should not be arrested in the first round.

As the police cars started to roll in—two, then four, then six—the cops were pointing us out and grouping us, presumably dividing up the arrestees. In the meantime, Brown started reading the Pottinger Settlement.

The minutes rolled on and the cops did not make a move. More supporters arrived to witness the scene and decide for themselves if it was for real. People gathered in small groups on the outskirts of the land, engaged in heated discussions about what was going on, the housing crisis and self-determination in the black community (they also discussed the white people erecting tents, but I did not hear those conversations personally). It was slowly turning into a circus.

We continued our work of cleaning up the lot and setting up tents. Food Not Bombs arrived, as promised, but we decided to resolve the situation with police before preparing any food. The neighborhood children were stricken by curiosity, so we assigned someone to childcare.

Suddenly, the cops huddled up, several of them eagerly pulling the flex cuffs from their rear pockets. I motioned to our people to brace for arrests and then listened in on the conversation. Brown did not speak, but another officer said that if there were no crimes being committed, their orders were to disperse.

The jaws in blue dropped.

"I said disperse."

The police peeled out of the circle, loaded the cruisers and left the lot. The people cheered.

OUR FIRST DONATION

The sight of the police pulling away made an impression on the neighbors and future residents, some of whom were on the edges of the property preparing to run from the impending raid and return to their park bench or spot under the bridge.

This was a real, tangible victory that the people witnessed with their own eyes. The new residents confidently returned to the center of the land, looking to contribute to the construction and food preparation.

The neighbors, in the meantime, engaged in an intense huddle, followed by a frenzy of activity. When the huddle broke, one of the neighbors, Tiffany, approached to inform me that the residents of the apartment had volunteered to help cook the first night's meal and that those same neighbors, living in dilapidated housing themselves, had taken a collection. With all the dignity she could muster, Tiffany handed me seven worn dollar bills. Our first donation. It was the biggest donation we would receive—not in dollar amount, but in sacrifice.

THE FIRST ATTACKS

The kitchen crew started preparing food. The crowds grew, including one woman who took one of our pieces of cardboard to draw a sign to protest us. Our supporters initially engaged her, but I urged them to let her express herself and even offered her some water. After half an hour, she left looking a bit discouraged.

The Liberty City Trust, formerly known as the Mode City Trust—the board entrusted to develop the very lot we took over, failing miserably and shamefully in the process—showed up to survey the situation. They were not pleased.

One of the board members, Roy Hardemon, showed up steaming mad along side local political hack Haneef Hamadullah. Roy is a Liberty City gadfly, a perennial candidate for one elected office or another, without ever cracking the 10% vote barrier.

Roy started cursing up a storm, declaring that the Liberty City Trust was just about to build something on that lot, a lot that had sat vacant for eight years. He complained bitterly that I was messing up his game and demanded I call the whole thing off and take down the tents. I was unable to completely stifle my laughter.

Haneef, in the meantime, was evidently ordered to scare participants from their task of building a city. This was nothing new for him, as several black elected officials had hired him as a political hit man. He has openly bragged about being paid by politicians to tear down campaign signs and verbally or physically disrupt meetings held by the opposition. He has been employed by Kendrick Meek, Carrie Meek, Dorothy Bendross Mindingall and, of course, Dorrin Rolle, among others.

Haneef ran around the lot dumping the contents of the trash bags we had filled, including needles, baggies, used condoms and empty bottles of alcohol. He yelled at people putting up tents or cooking. His antics were not limited to that day; once the Village was established, he often drove his pickup onto the land at five in the morning, honking his horn non-stop for minutes at a time.

One day, Haneef got out of his truck to yell at people and our neighbors yelled back at him. In response, Haneef pulled down his pants to expose himself to them and two young girls before driving away with his "Re-Elect Dorrin Rolle" stickers on his truck. Miami police initially refused to take a police report until we repeated the part about the school-aged children and hinted at taking the story to the media instead.

Roy Hardemon started planting dark blue "Jim Davis for Governor" yard signs on the land. During this moment of black self-determination, it was nothing short of shameful to watch Roy promote the Democratic Party's great white hope gubernatorial candidate in order to detract from a people's movement.

While Roy worked his way around the lot, someone removed most of the planted signs. Roy dialed 911.

Roy demanded the police arrest me and four others for the destruction of his personal property. As the police begin investigating the crime, interviewing suspects and witnesses, Haneef reported that someone was "stealing" the contents of the trash bags he dumped on the ground. The cops refused to arrest anyone for picking up trash or Haneef for dumping it. After an hour-long investigation, the police informed Roy there was not enough evidence to arrest anyone for the removal of his "Davis for Governor" signs.

The war of words raged on until dark. The police remained on the scene ostensibly to keep the peace, but their main active duty consists of keeping Roy and Haneef—the ones who called the police in the first place—away from people minding their own business and building a city.

Poncho was incredible as the police liaison. She asserted our positions well, while maintaining her professional demeanor, which kept things cool. She negotiated the political space we needed and was able to make lightning-quick assessments of the situation on an ongoing basis. At the end of the day, her counterpart on the police force sought Poncho out to suggest that she would make a great police dispatcher or community relations person and that the department was hiring.

Later, while making the rounds, I paused to listen in as one of the high-ranking officers explained the official police position. He said that I and the others were protesting the housing scandal, and would be there tonight and maybe tomorrow night making our point, and then things would get back to normal. I smiled and walked away.

BUILDING THE CITY

The Lake Worth Kids and other anarchists did an amazing job of building a small city. They were efficient, organized (yes, organized anarchists) and dedicated. Their focus on the logistical tasks at hand left the Black Response free to handle police, community and media relations. The fact is we could not have built units or prepared food without them, and we can never possibly thank them adequately. I can only hope that this mention reveals our gratitude, however insufficiently expressed.

Amanda Seaton took on a variety of tasks throughout the day, seizing and solving problems independently and brilliantly. Given her previously-expressed skepticism, her jumping from a bit role to that of a major participant was a welcome surprise.

I burned up cell phone minutes seeking advice from our lawyers, Ray Taseff and Benji Waxman. Julia Dawson, a trusted confidant and one of South Florida's leading feminist activists, served as our legal observer in just one of her significant contributions to the action. As the first plates of food were being served, I was formally introduced to one of our new residents, shaking hands for the first time with Jonathan Baker, who would emerge as our most outspoken, and well spoken, resident, rising to the defense of the Village over and again.

Perhaps it should not have been so surprising, but virtually everything worked as planned. Most importantly, a community witnessed the first volley in a real land struggle in the U.S. Because the concept was accessible and the local benefits of the land takeover were tangible—building a shantytown for the local homeless population—people believed in the idea and that this was the right solution to the problem. Believed that we could, and should, do this.

As darkness took hold, residents, neighbors, volunteers and supporters gathered on a plot of land that had stood vacant for eight long years, but was now to be put to use for the benefit of the community. Somehow, Bernadette and I were able to steal a few moments together.

We rallied on the land. Volunteers and residents spoke and supporters delivered messages of solidarity. Eventually, I made my way to the makeshift stage, marveling at the land, the people and the movement. We passed our first big test and it was right to celebrate and claim victory.

"Welcome to liberated land. This is what it feels like to be free..."

After building the kitchen, we built shanties out of wooden pallets. We attracted new residents on a daily basis and struggled to erect units quickly enough to house them all. Media, visitors, sightseers and volunteers came to the land to witness the shantytown for themselves. People were shocked, yet moved and inspired to contribute and help their fellow human beings who were attempting to help themselves.

The residents learned to build shanties and were responsible for security, cleaning up, preparing food and every other aspect of maintaining their homes. Every Thursday night, we sat in the living room—an assortment of couches—and engaged in political education. The organizers learned as much as the residents, if not more.

Two weeks after the founding, and after internal discussion, we invited our supporters to the official naming ceremony. We were now the Umoja Village.

Compost toilet, the shower with ladder
and water bucket and a garden.

Residents often prayed together before
meals.

The meal line.

7. The Adversarial Takeover of Land

EVEN MORE IMPORTANT THAN the logistical plans for taking land and building the shantytown, were the ideological and political underpin-

nings guiding the decision. Due to the broad nature of the strategic partnership planning and implementing the action, the political framing for
the action was equally broad.

One of the most powerful aspects of the action was that inside of that
broad framework, each individual and group was free to bring their own
priorities and ideology, and each set of ideas carried as much value and
legitimacy in relationship to the action as the others.

So, while some of us approached the land takeover as a function of Pan-
Africanism in one of its diasporic manifestations, others saw it as the ful-
fillment of a particular form of nationalism, while others considered it part
of the movement to prioritize the earth, re-establishing the relationship
between people and the land. Each view contained value and significance
and, for our purposes, no single perspective dominated over another.

Every coalition demands some level of political unity, and for the purposes
of building the shantytown, we more than achieved the requisite standards.

It should be made clear that while the level of unity we achieved proved
ideal for this strategic partnership, it is not necessarily sufficient for other
formations, including political organizations and certain types of coalitions. Under other circumstances, more rigorous levels of political unity
must be achieved prior to moving on such a substantial initiative.

For better or for worse, the problems associated with lacking political
unity are rarely evident when an action fails; they are, instead, revealed
after achieving a certain level of success, when participants must determine the next logical steps, and it is during those next steps that dormant
issues often come to life.

For example, in the 1950s and 60s, opposing Jim Crow and segregation
provided sufficient unity for organizations and individuals to participate
in the civil rights movement. However, only upon achieving certain levels
of success—specifically, ending legal segregation—did the lack of deeper
political and ideological unity emerge as a significant factor.

After the fall of Jim Crow laws, some believed their mission was accomplished and disconnected from the broader social justice movement.
Others shifted focus towards maximizing gains for the black middle class
through municipal and other middle-management jobs. Others pursued
the end of the economic Jim Crow which gave teeth to the political system of discrimination. Still others considered the fall of Jim Crow a prerequisite in the multi-stepped march towards African Liberation.

The strategic partnership built by Take Back the Land, on the other
hand, worked because we achieved the level of political unity required

for the action, the political leadership was clearly identified and respected, and the strategic partners were given space to do their work, without unnecessary and unneeded demonstration of "leadership."

PRINCIPLES OF UNITY

The ideas that bound a loose band of activists from a broad range of backgrounds and ideologies formed the framework upon which political unity was built. We agreed on a core set of axioms or principles of unity, including:

- There is a crisis of gentrification and housing.
- Housing, food and living in dignity are human rights.
- The root of the crisis is greed, and as long as profits are prioritized over people, and the exploitation of people and natural resources is a primary means of generating profit, the crisis will continue.
- Development is about people, not buildings or profits.
- The solution to the problem is community control over land. Each community must determine the best use of their own land.
- The black community must control land in the black community.
- We have a collective right to the land and an obligation as stewards of the land.
- The government is part of the problem, and, therefore, we cannot depend on them to be part of the solution.
- People must control their own lives. Self-determination is an integral part of liberation.

While race was not a major part of the axioms, there was plenty of room inside of those principles for individuals to advance their own hard race-based line. In the same way, there was space for a hard environmentalist line as well as lines in which economic analysis was primary.

Another important concept not explicitly listed was the idea that even as we took control over land, it did not "belong" to us, it belonged to the indigenous people of this continent, those commonly called Indians. Many, but not all, of us held that land stolen five hundred years ago is still stolen land. As such, we were honored to welcome Sheridan Murphy of the American Indian Movement (AIM) who blessed the land on behalf of its rightful owners.

Again, while this arrangement functioned for this particular formation, in which there was a lot of trust among the actors and a clear project plan and objectives, it will not necessarily work in every scenario. Objective analysis of each situation will determine the best political formation, given the participants and realities on the ground.

POLITICAL OBJECTIVES

We recognized the need to develop clear political objectives in order to accomplish two things: first, to establish, in advance, guiding principles by which we could solve unforeseen problems and make decisions about next steps.

Political objectives provide commonly agreed-upon goal lines, toward which participants advanced. When forced to make big decisions or to regroup, the objectives gave us context and orientation around which we could regain our footing.

Further, because we empowered participants to make a range of decisions, the established principles and objectives enabled individuals to make decisions by simply applying those principles and objectives to any given situation. Those decisions which advanced our objectives and remained inside of our principles were good ones.

For example, if a government official dropped by unannounced to offer residents temporary shelter in exchange for quitting the land, anyone could easily apply our principles and objectives and reject the offer without having to check back with the group.

The second benefit to developing clear political objectives lay in providing us, and the community, with a measuring stick through which we could evaluate successes and failures. Without pre-determined objectives, one can easily make bad deals and then claim easy victories. These claims can only be made in the absence of objective pre-existing standards by which to measure the deal or "victory."

Conversely, political objectives helped us realize victory even when it felt like defeat. For example, dealing with fifty people, many with social, chemical and/or mental health issues, is extremely challenging. Three months into the project, the constant personality clashes and ongoing management issues might convince people that they are in the midst of a historic failure. However, the only objective way to evaluate the proximity to victory or defeat is by measuring the objective reality against the political objectives.

In any event, three primary political objectives of the project were hammered out, with concepts or sub-objectives or strategies associated with each. The objectives were:

- House and feed people.
- Assert the right of the black community to control land in the black community.
- Build a new society.

1. HOUSE AND FEED PEOPLE

At first blush, this objective appeared so rudimentary and obvious that we almost did not include it at all. In one sense, we accomplished this objective on October 23, 2006 when we arrived on the lot and housed and fed several homeless people. On a deeper level, we continuously struggled to meet this objective, and all of its implications, each and every day.

This objective is the lowest, in terms of political content, easiest to measure and one around which the greatest number of people could unify, including everyone who visited and contributed to the Umoja Village. This fact is important because it enabled us to secure material support from people who we might not otherwise have coaxed into assisting us, people who might not have agreed with me personally or with some of our other objectives.

While some commented on or did not fully understand our other objectives, virtually everyone believed in the human right to housing and food, and our human obligation to provide those needs to our sisters and brothers. There has been no better rallying point, particularly among those who did not understand our broader political objectives or those who did not embrace them.

This objective also guided our decision making on a practical level. As the number of residents began to swell, the challenges associated with feeding more than forty people three times per day, seven days a week grew as well. It rapidly became clear that continued unsustainable growth threatened the entire project, presenting challenges of logistics, human relations and security—as provocateurs, obviously sent by our detractors, appeared from time to time.

Personally knowing each of our residents and discussing the political context of the Village was critical in terms of creating a sense of ownership, buy-in and unity, a process that resulted in residents volunteering to maintain the village as well as refraining from activities that could result in its destruction.

Also, as we surpassed forty residents, our food supplies would occasionally diminish. This reality on the micro level was useful in demonstrating to our residents the importance of protecting and behaving responsibly with our natural resources on the macro level.

The decision to stop building was painful and difficult, especially for those who slept on the couch waiting for the next shanties to be built. But given our objectives, the correct decision was obvious, even if difficult. In order to house and feed those we currently supported, we had to limit our growth, at least until our resources grew. Or until we liberated more land...

In a broader sense, we have an obligation to house and feed our sisters and brothers. The fact that the government is unable or unwilling to co-ordinate and facilitate that process does not alleviate us of our responsibility, in fact, quite the opposite: it heightens our responsibility because the social contract engineered to meet those obligations is breached. We were meeting our obligations to our people.

2. ASSERT THE RIGHT OF THE BLACK COMMUNITY TO CONTROL LAND IN THE BLACK COMMUNITY

The higher political objective, and the one with which Take Back the Land is most closely associated, is the assertion that the land in the black community belongs to the black community and, therefore, must be controlled by the black community.

Inherent in this assertion is a recognition of two realities: first, we do not control the land in the neighborhoods in which we live. The powers-that-be, either in the form of wealthy developers or the government which advances the interests of those same wealthy developers, controls the land in our community. Overwhelmingly, those wealthy interests are non-black people controlling the land in black communities. Further, those dual powers conspire to maintain control over our land so that they can continue to reap the benefits, invariably at our expense.

The second inherent reality in the assertion is that in spite of the exploitation and oppression that denies us control over the land, it is ultimately our own responsibility to gain that control as a means of solving the problems plaguing us.

If wealthy interests and the government that works for them want to profit from our resources, no amount of begging, marching, singing or appeals to moral conscience will convince them to give up their profits so that oppressed people might benefit. If they were so inclined, they probably would not be oppressing us so much in the first place. Whoever is the cause of the problem, we are responsible for the solution and we must behave as such.

This assertion and objective is at the heart of the land question. Land in our community is routinely taken and used for the benefit of members of other communities, the standard operating procedure in colonial type relationships—and black communities in the U.S. are essentially domestic colonies, serving as centers for low-wage labor and a market for cheap goods.

In the midst of a crisis of gentrification and low-income housing, wealthy, politically-connected developers were getting land in the black community at fire sale prices, and often for free. The land giveaway allowed the developers to maximize their own profits, while deepening the ongoing crisis of gentrification and housing in the black community.

The solution to this problem cannot be found in the halls of power, which sanction and facilitate the exploitative relationship in the first place. The solution to the problem lies in the black community exercising control over the land, politics and economy of our communities.

Via collective control over land, as opposed to individual ownership of land, communities can make decisions about land use that benefit the community itself, not individual land or business owners whose pursuit of profit is a stronger pull than the commitment to broader social justice imperatives.

Because key players in municipal governments—and in the federal government as well—are bankrolled in one form or another by major financial interests, and because those elected into office overwhelmingly share the same class interests as those same financial interests, local governments work for big money, not for the average person.

Miami provides the perfect example. Mayor Manny Diaz's election campaigns are bankrolled by big developers. Diaz himself is a developer. When he thinks about an issue, he not only thinks about it as a developer because he is one, but thinks about it in terms of the interests of developers because they are the ones to whom he is politically beholden.

The same is true of his lackey on the Miami Commission, Michelle Spence-Jones. Her election campaign financing is derived almost exclusively from the Diaz political machine. When deciding how to vote, she must first consider the will of those who put her in power: Manny Diaz and his developer friends. The same applies to Miami-Dade Commissioner, and notorious sell-out, Dorrin Rolle.

The land, then, in the black community, is largely controlled by one of two forces: either wealthy developers/landlords who buy cheap property and maintain slum conditions as part of their business model, or by local governments who operate on behalf of the interests of the wealthy developers.

In the final analysis, developers have money, own land and employ government officials to fight for their interests. The black community has little money, even less land and few fighting for its interests.

What we do have, however, is our labor. In this context "labor" is not limited to what we sell to business owners in exchange for an hourly wage, but includes our ability to take the streets in a fight for our rights.

In addition, the collective control over land invokes the concept of self-determination, in the political sense. The black community must develop a collective vision and muster the collective will and power to realize that vision. Because it does not exist in reality, the invoked concept of self-determination is a central part of the third objective.

3. BUILD A NEW SOCIETY

The idea of building a new society is so simple, it is profound.

On any other corner, poor, black homeless people, particularly women, are on the margins of society's margins. They have no political power, their opinions do not matter and more effort is exerted by the state to dislocate or hide them than to assist them.

As we engaged in discussions about the concept of organizing the homeless, time and again we were told that they qualify as the most difficult group to organize. Some are not in full control of their faculties, for one reason or another, and suffer under the dual scourge of mental illness and hard core drug addiction.

And yet, we assert that the most marginal members of society are better qualified to run their "city" or "village" than the college-educated elected official and bureaucrat. We not only asserted the proposition, we proved it as Umoja's residents made real decisions about the rules of the Village and the manner in which it was run.

In this new society, people not only related differently to the land itself, they related differently to one another and, ultimately, to power—they had all of it while on the land.

Residents literally interacted differently with each other while on the land than while off, even just a few blocks away. While it was difficult to completely negate the years of conditioning imposed on people from the broader society, the idea that we were building something new and different captured the imagination of our residents and supporters in a real and lasting way.

In this new society human beings are valued over and above material things, creature comforts and even profit.

Residents relax and socialize.

Neighbors provided electricity to the village.

Mamyrah introduces Jungle Queen.

8. Building Umoja

THERE ARE TWO CATEGORIES of homeless: the street homeless and the under-housed. While most are familiar with the street homeless, including the chronically homeless, the under-housed population is almost totally invisible. The under-housed are not living on the street, but do not have a place of their own, often due to the lack of affordable housing.

During a housing crunch, individuals and families are often forced to double and triple up in the homes of their relatives. The overcrowding, and the turn of events that led to the overcrowding in the first place, are a source of great tension in the household. Equally as stressful is the fact that because the additional family members are not on the lease, the arrangement threatens the housing security of everyone involved.

People are placed in the unenviable position of choosing between standing idly by while their relatives are put out on the street or taking those relatives in and risking eviction themselves. In public housing, the additional relatives often are forced to wait until after 5:00PM, when government workers leave their posts, before going "home." Children are unable to go indoors or study until the government officials leave for the day, under the risk of evicting their entire extended family.

When planning the Village, we fully expected to attract the street homeless, but were surprised at the number of under-housed residents who came to live at Umoja in order to buy themselves time and space.

During the majority of our tenure, approximately half of the residents worked, mostly full-time minimum wage jobs, and several went to school. Some of the residents had been just "one paycheck away" from homelessness and lost that paycheck. Free housing and food allowed many of them to regain that paycheck and peace of mind.

The Umoja Village residents were an eclectic and fascinating group. Several young couples, with one or both working, moved into Umoja, and many of our elder residents had incredible stories to tell.

A young lovestruck Latino couple, both of whom worked menial jobs, lived on the sands of Miami Beach, but could not afford housing. After hearing about Umoja on the radio, they grabbed their backpacks and walked almost six miles to the land. The lovebirds were always holding hands and flirting, and took great care to fix up their shanty like home, including a welcome mat, carpeting and a family portrait. Because they did not have to purchase restaurant food for three meals a day, and they could store some goods, they were able to save money and eventually moved out of Miami.

When Darryl arrived on the land, there were no available shanties, so he secured a spot on the waiting list and slept on the couch for nearly two weeks. As big as he was, Darryl could not help with construction because his right arm was in a sling, permanently injured due to an accident. He immediately volunteered to organize the kitchen and clothing storage space, keeping it neat and in order at all times. The residents, who decided on expansion and move-ins during Sunday Meetings, found him so indispensable that he was moved to the front of the waiting list and scored the next available unit.

Darryl just needed a little time to get himself together, and that he did. As social service organizations came, he applied for numerous housing options and was finally accepted. Even after moving out of Umoja and up to an apartment, he returned to the land twice a week to volunteer his time. He eventually joined LIFFT and continues to fight for social justice.

Many older residents, such as Simeon and Mr. Fredrick, worked. Most others, however—like Junior, Lanish, and Roosevelt—received pensions or social security, but the housing crisis ensured their homelessness.

T-Bone was a hard worker with an easy self-depreciating demeanor, and was as honest as they come, a challenging feat for someone who is not guaranteed a meal on a daily basis. T-Bone continued to contribute greatly to the organization, in word and deed. I also grew very fond of Shabazz, whose potential was limitless. Shabazz was in his early 30s and was an intelligent, well read, thoughtful and sensitive man. When dressed up, you could easily think you were talking to a lawyer, banker or other professional. Shabazz and I are still close to this day; I appreciate our time together.

Much like our under-housed population, it seemed clear that most of the chronically homeless Umoja residents would not be homeless if they only had access to appropriate and quality social services, particularly mental health services. Cheryl Orange was involved with political organizations in her younger years, a story we cannot fully piece together due to her mental illness. We discovered a longtime resident received a sizable monthly pension, enough to afford housing and care, but was unable to access it without consistent support from a caseworker—support he only received when the government had a greater interest in moving him, and others, out of Umoja than in his remaining neglected.

Above all, Umoja residents were extremely proud, a characteristic which blossomed during their experience there.

JOHN CATA

According to the *Miami Herald*, and to anyone who would listen, in 1968 during a time of heated political and union activism, a young, spry John Cata negotiated and signed the first union contract between the workers at Jackson Memorial, Miami-Dade's public hospital, and the county government, which employed them. The following year, in what he believes was a political induction resulting from his activism, Cata was drafted and shipped to Vietnam to serve a tour of duty, allegedly to fight for the right of the Vietnamese to enjoy privileges there that Cata, and other black people, could not even exercise themselves here.

Shortly after Christmas 2006, returning from one of his regular treks to the downtown library, this same John Cata—a bit older and a lot wiser—finally decided to stop by the shantytown he passed daily on the way to and from "home." He introduced himself, was offered and partook in food, engaged in stimulating conversation and decided he liked it at Umoja. He walked a few blocks away, retrieved his belongings and moved into Umoja Village.

John Cata was nothing short of an historic figure in Miami-Dade County. And yet, prior to moving into Umoja, he had been living behind bushes in a vacant lot in Liberty City. With all he did for the county and the country that conscripted his service, few favors were forthcoming in return.

Cata immediately fit in and contributed insightful suggestions about political direction, strategies and tactics. He was an engaging man, with piercing eyes and a story for every possible occasion.

His storytelling provided a great frame as he fixed up his shanty and made it like a regular house. He purchased linoleum and tiled his floor, planted a garden and added patio furniture. He erected a white picket fence, with functional gate, around his shanty, in homage to his late mother, who was never able to erect her white picket fence in her apartment in Queens, NY. Cata's home was a full tourist attraction.

He charmed his way into multiple speaking engagements, including at Florida International University and the University of Miami. He was sharp as a tack, even if his temper was quick to blow.

Cata was the first to sign up for our actions during the week the Super Bowl came to Miami, logging the first arrest in his sixty-four years, as we moved him and another family into chronically vacant public housing units. He was a media hit, and well respected in the Village.

And yet, he was otherwise homeless.

When his story is written, in whatever form, it will not speak kindly of the wealthiest country in the history of planet Earth that John Cata was sucked into homelessness.

THE DAY THE FOOD RAN OUT

In the early days of the Umoja Village, we were way ahead of the curve in achieving our most challenging objective: creating a new society. Even with our problems, residents were genuinely happy, participated in daily life on the land and treated the land and resources with respect. This was particularly the case when dealing with donations.

Donations were taken into the pantry or storage, food was shared and distributed, and oftentimes the common courtesy displayed was almost uncommon. On more than one occasion, one resident would pick out some food or article of clothing and when another resident expressed interest in the item, the first resident, an otherwise homeless person with meager personal belongings, shared or gave the item up.

At times, our donations were so solid that a car full of fresh, hot food often failed to stir the residents' passions. They would look at the food and return to their business, whether debating the latest hot topic, working on the land or back at the task of doing nothing in particular.

There was so much food security, that security was almost completely unnecessary. Neither the pantry nor the storage room had doors and any hungry person, resident or transient, was free to walk into the kitchen and make themselves some food at any time of the day or night.

The fact that a group of people could exist and thrive in the middle of an inner city ghetto with no doors or other security to protect their valuables is a testament to the extent to which tendencies towards greed and hoarding are socialized, learned behaviors, not inherent traits of humans in general, or black people in particular. The fact that this same group was comprised of otherwise homeless individuals, some of whom were living with a drug addiction that otherwise compelled them to steal, is testament to the socially calming effects of food and housing security, coupled with participatory, bottom-up democracy.

In other words, if you want to end street level crime in inner city communities, a society can either try to arrest every black person in sight, or it can fundamentally undermine the purposes and objectives of the crime. Want people to stop stealing for food, clothing and shelter? Give them food, clothing and shelter. Want to stop oppressed people from anti-social behavior, which expresses their sense of alienation? Stop oppressing them, and allow them to make real decisions about the their own collective destiny.

At Umoja, the abundance of food and goods—as well as the obvious love the community, organizers and volunteers had for the residents and the project—created a sense of hope that probably did not previously exist, either in the residents or the participants. There was genuine excitement about what we were doing, and that excitement was contagious and facilitated the leap of faith so many residents made, leaving the 'deficit consciousness' behind and working collectively towards building a new society.

All of that came to a crashing halt one weekday afternoon.

Three factors clashed during a short time frame: first, donations dropped off a bit and the organizers failed to put out a new call for more. Second, our numbers continued to swell, as we grew beyond forty residents. Additionally, neighbors and other passersby pulled and tugged at our finite resources. And third, someone(s), resident or transient, was pilfering modest amounts of food from the pantry. Any one of those factors alone could not have triggered a crisis, but all three conspired together as one day, for a few short hours, we totally and completely ran out of food.

In all likelihood, one or two residents walked into the pantry, assessed the food supply and made a business decision to ensure that they would eat over the next several days, even if no one else did. Once the pantry was barren, a sense of panic overtook every resident who walked in and found it empty.

It is difficult to explain, but when I pulled up to the Village that day, there was a noticeable change in the collective mood. I did not, at the time, fully appreciate the change, but I did notice it right away. Residents huddled in small groups, whispering and plotting and even looking at me differently, not greeting me in the usual friendly way. The sense of serenity which had once hovered over the encampment gave way to a general sense of unease. Many of the residents physically looked as if they were back on the streets, no longer in their maroon society of peace and love. Something in their eyes betrayed a sense of panic.

I became curious enough to ask what was going on, and was informed of the food situation. Because I had been monitoring the inventory, I was a bit surprised that supplies had run out so quickly—hence my subsequent piecing together of the last moments of the pantry formerly known as full—but was not at all surprised that we had run out of food. Without thinking too much about it, I announced that we would purchase food for the night's meal and resumed my routine of inspection, inquiring about incidents, etc.

We had anticipated this eventuality and set aside funds specifically for such an occasion. Up until that time—this was mid-to-late January—the only food we had ever purchased were eggs for breakfast and ice to preserve all of the donated meat. However, what for me meant a simple administrative matter of using earmarked funds to purchase unprepared food meant something entirely different to the residents. Because I was not a resident and my personal food supply was not dependent upon the status of the pantry, I failed to recognize the clear signs of panic and change in the minds and hearts of our people.

After dinner was prepared and served by the residents, several people complained that they did not get enough, or any, food—the first such complaint I received there. I accepted responsibility for not purchasing enough food, unaware that the deficit consciousness, which promotes the hoarding of resources and the advancement of one's own lot at the expense of others', had returned with a vengeance in the collective consciousness of the residents.

For the next several days, after great responses to our call for donations, we simply could not purchase or receive enough food, and we ran out every single day, exacerbating an already serious crisis.

Residents complained bitterly that so-and-so was hoarding food, and there were days' worth of food loaded up in individual rooms while the pantry sat empty. For the first time, some residents—particularly the elderly, who could not fight so hard for their share of new donations—went hungry all day, while others had so much food that it literally rotted in their rooms, enjoyed only by the maggots.

It was fairly easy to see why the old rules of the street regained their appeal. Food and supplies were disappearing, and those kind enough to allow someone before them in the food line did not always eat. Under those circumstances, it was not unreasonable to conclude that one should get for themselves while the getting is still there. While this conclusion appears reasonable, it dooms everyone involved.

The more sophisticated vision of the Village and, by extension, the entire world, is that there are adequate resources, so long as one takes what they need right now, not what they want over the next week or two. I am certain that the rotted uneaten food would have been sufficient to feed everyone left wanting, if only it had been made available to them. In the same respect, uneaten food in the U.S., even just the leftovers trashed in expensive restaurants, is surely enough to put a serious dent in the global crisis of hunger.

Choosing collective resource management over individual hoarding was the only legitimate means of managing resources on the land. However, it only works when practiced by the majority.

The same applies to capitalism in the broader context. The world produces adequate resources to house, clothe, feed and provide medical care for every human on earth. The reason why everyone does not eat everyday, on Umoja and on earth, is because a small number of people hoard resources, either in their mansions or in their shanty, and literally throw away more food than others consume.

But there is a clear double standard when applying the principle of shared resources to the white first world and to poor black people. Poor welfare mothers are vilified by politicians and the press for arranging to receive a few extra dollars per month in benefits, but corporate welfare recipients are never blamed for taking money from social services. In the same way, it is easy to cast blame on the "greedy" homeless people who hoard cans of beans and styrofoam containers of food in their shanties while other homeless people go hungry, but no one blames the greedy who consume food, water, energy and entertainment above and beyond their percentage of the world's population, while millions starve to death in other parts of the world.

Back at Umoja, the hoarding mentality raged out of control. For the first time, there was real stealing of food from the kitchen. As a consequence, the residents were highly agitated and during Sunday Meeting took the unprecedented step of setting opening and closing hours on the kitchen. Those individuals—residents and transients—who violated the rules and were caught, were dealt with in one way or another.

The new rules made it more difficult for desperate residents to get away with jostling for position in the food line or pilfering a few extra cans from the pantry, and so the battlefield moved. As cars pulled up, residents moved to get first dibs on the donations. In some cases, it became a mob scene at the car of unsuspecting donors. Before the goods were unloaded from the car and walked to the table, people were fighting over the food or clothes. Some visitors were spooked and never returned.

In the end, residents voted to purchase locks and install doors on the kitchen and storage room. One key was given to Poncho and another to a resident responsible for opening and closing the rooms at pre-established times. The transition to the new way of doing things took some time, but the residents eventually adjusted and the process worked smoothly.

The real damage, however, was inflicted upon the idealistic model of building a new society, one with no locks or doors, even in the context of intense poverty. The image of the locked double doors was much harder on me than it was on the residents. Something changed and the reality was that we had made incredible strides towards building a new society, however, we were not yet there.

In response to the chaos, we organized donations so that they were delivered during predictable times when organizers were present to reassure residents and ensure the calm and orderly distribution of resources. In practice, when cars rolled up, we assigned one or two residents to retrieve the donations, and assured the other residents they would have access to them.

Residents voted on feeding the elderly first during meal times, and it was the role of the organizers to assure that occurred. The organizers did not start cooking or serving, but we did make sure the lines were formed and kept properly. More importantly than the logistics of the line, we reassured the residents that there was enough food for everyone—and there almost always was—and that everyone would get their fair share if we took only what we needed.

The efforts paid off, as in a few weeks—although it seemed like a few months—the donation mobs subsided and the food supply normalized. Kinks persisted, particularly when new people arrived who were not oriented towards the new society, but nothing like the day food ran out.

In retrospect, we erred in assuming that because residents loved the Village and their new life there, including the abundance of food, they fully internalized the concepts of collectivism. In reality, collectivism worked for them because there was plenty of food, not because the principles were fully internalized. That assumption caused us to skip the important steps of providing the political leadership and cultural reinforcement necessary in building the new society.

People who believe in a concept, believe in it when it works as well as when it does not work so hot. People who believe in God thank Her when good happens, and continue to believe when bad happens. That is the result of both faith and understanding. We had not built a strong enough understanding of the concepts of the new society to weather the test in faith and understanding that was sure to accompany our first crisis in resources.

WHAT'S IN A NAME

After settling on "Umoja Village," we constantly engaged in the process of naming ourselves, both for the land and for the residents.

We used "residents" almost by default, failing to come up with something better. Not many alternatives existed, but then what were our options? "The Umojans" made it sound as if we were from another planet, and there were clear copyright issues at stake in using "The Village People."

Conversely, there was no shortage of aliases for Umoja. The most common among activists and the broader community was "The Land." That said it all, was extremely powerful and spoke to the primacy of land as our political statement. Informally, we also called it "the spot" ("you going to the spot?"), "the Village," "shantytown" and a host of other predictable names.

Unbeknownst to me, the neighbors (another name for the apartment next door to the land) gave us a name of their own: "Smallville." Poncho first broke the news, but I was unsure as to whether to believe her.

One day I was talking to Clayton, one of the neighbors, as he recounted an issue they were having with one of our residents. Much like one of the Sunday Meetings at Umoja, the neighbors had gathered, had a meeting and voted to banish the guy from the apartment complex.

Clayton recalled telling him, "'you can't come around here no more. You have to stay in Smallville."

I'm still unsure whether to be appreciative or offended.

RONNIE HOLMES

Ronnie Holmes was absolutely brilliant. Even during informal side conversations, it was easy to see his mind at work and appreciate his wit and intelligence. His analysis was sharp and cutting, his public speaking skills were top notch and his ability to roll up his sleeves and get to work was envied by other residents.

Ronnie Holmes was also addicted to crack. When jonesing, he would lie, rob and steal without thinking about it twice. The contrast between his visionary political analysis and his personal behavior was deep and disturbing. The power of drug addiction and the harshness of his life was written in brutal bold print across his face.

Ronnie—or Rock, as he was known on the street—came to Umoja on the second or third day. He looked around and absorbed the vibe in total wide-eyed wonder. He was first inspired and then became inspiring. After his first night at Umoja, Ronnie returned to his spot under the bridge to gather his belongings and transport them to his new home. After picking up his bag, he suddenly stopped short, reached into his pocket, pulled out a crack pipe and tossed it. "I won't be needing that anymore."

Ronnie represents the dilemma of being young, gifted and black in America. As smart and talented as he was, Ronnie, like many other black males in the U.S., was reduced to a summation of his worse characteristics: a hustling drug addict.

During Sunday Meetings, Ronnie was proactive and full of good suggestions, as well as his fair share of pie-in-the-sky ideas. He earned the respect of his fellow residents and established himself as a leader. Ronnie spoke at press conferences—ours and those of our allies—and waxed poetic in front of guests. We became close friends as he struggled to reinvent himself and use his talents to benefit his home and his larger community.

He was proud of his picture on the front page of the *Miami Times* where he was prominently quoted. Later that week, Ronnie was reunited with his long lost son after the child's mother saw Ronnie in the newspaper. Ronnie Holmes, tough guy, wept openly on the land.

In the midst of respect and growing accolades, the addiction started pushing back, and he began to use, rarely at first, but steadily, and noticeably, increasing. At the beginning, he was remarkably self aware. During Sunday Meetings, as we discussed locking up the kitchen, Ronnie made some of the best security suggestions, as a means of protecting his beloved land from his alter ego, a split personality he hated, but had come to accept as his own personal reality.

"I'm a crackhead," Ronnie announced fervently, but as if he were talking about someone else. "We have to put extra wood on the back window of the kitchen to keep me out of there at night."

Less than a week later, in the heat of the night, the sound of breaking wood aroused the residents to the sight of someone trying to break into the kitchen in search of valuables to feed their habit. Ronnie the crack addict was thwarted by the only one smart enough to outwit him: Brilliant Ronnie. His own security suggestion ultimately earned him three days off the land.

Ronnie was arrested, off the land, and jailed for less than thirty days. Upon his release Ronnie returned, but his behavior was more erratic and the fine balance between his brilliant and drug-addicted egos was shattered. Far from being "corrected," his addiction seemed to intensify in jail, making him more unstable. He was suspended from the land on multiple occasions, until he was finally voted off for good.

Less than one month into his exile from the land, and less than four months after reuniting with his son—with whom he frequently visited and even assisted with homework—Ronnie Holmes was shot dead in the street less than a mile from the Umoja Village.

The news hit me, and the Village, like a ton of bricks and compelled introspection around the impact of drugs on our communities. How many of our bright young women and men have fallen victim to the plague? The reflection led me to three angry conclusions.

First, the consequences of drug use in the context of social oppression and degradation is disproportionate to the consequences in other contexts. When poor black men use drugs, they end up arrested or dead on the street. When rich white men abuse drugs, their fathers get them elected president. If Ronnie Holmes and George W. Bush were to trade places, Ronnie would be a smart president and George W. never would have lived long enough to see the Umoja Village. Say what you will about taking personal responsibility, but rich white kids are not compelled to carry the same burden because they are constantly bailed out by their parents, their money, their connections and a society that is far more forgiving of them than of black males.

Second, Ronnie's life was tragically short, both in span and in realized potential; however, it is difficult to determine who is the worse as a result. Is it him for not living long or well enough; his children, denied a potentially wonderful father; or the broader society, denied the benefits of Ronnie's insight, genius and contributions?

When someone fails to realize their potential, everyone loses, albeit for slightly different reasons. By the same token, when an entire segment of the population is marginalized, and therefore fails to reach their potential, the implications are devastating: for that segment, the broader population, and indeed, the entire planet.

When one human being oppresses another, the oppressed suffers in obvious ways, but the oppressor, and those who sit by passively, also suffer because they lose the benefit of human potential. We need this human potential, and I am angry that Ronnie Holmes is not by our side right now fighting for land. The loss is made greater by knowing that were he not poor and black, in all probability, he would still be among us.

The third conclusion is that blacks are consistently defined by our faults, not our glories. Ronnie was both a brilliant man and a tragic figure. However, black people are not regarded in all our complexity, our highs and our lows, but instead reduced to the product of our lows.

Columbus is not recalled as a genocidal maniac, George Washington is not remembered as a slave owner and George W. Bush is not introduced as a drunk or drug addict. But so many complex—beautiful and ugly—black lives are reduced to "crackheads" or "criminals" and the like.

While Ronnie deserves to rest in peace, none of us alive should do so as long as human potential is disregarded like so much trash.

KNOW WHEN TO HOLD 'EM

Our first major internal crisis did not come as the result of a raid or a breakdown of our new society, but rather as a result of our incredible success.

As previously revealed, we expected a raid of some sort, if not immediately following the land seizure, then shortly thereafter, before we solidified our power. However, because of the extremity of the housing crisis and the strength of our support, the raid never came and we continued to build power. This was the source of our first major crisis.

Because our long-term trajectory had been largely based on the assumption that we would get raided, the lack of a raid left us in a bit of a bind in terms of determining our ultimate direction. As such, we had to decide what we were fundamentally there to do—to provoke a political crisis or to provide long term housing for people.

A critical component of direct action is using your tactics to provoke a political crisis, forcing the system to respond. This is exactly what Dr. King sought to accomplish during his actions, using provocative marches or sit-ins and non-violence as a tactic. Don't believe me, take one of the courses on his tactics.

If our fundamental objective was to provoke a crisis, we had to force the government to react to our presence. However, were building too much power and community support to achieve that objective. Our roots were deepening and it was looking like they would not be able to raid us.

So, we debated, discussed and argued: do we grow increasingly provocative? Do we take over more land? Or, do we hold what we have and solidify our position?

In the end, and primarily out of respect and love for our residents, we decided our fundamental objective was to provide housing, not to provoke the political crisis. Umoja lived on, largely unaware of how close we had come to provoking a crisis that might have ended it all.

Jewel Parham speaks as
Jonathan Baker waits in the wings.

General Rashid speaks during
the six-month anniversary celebration.

Amanda and Mamyrah demonstrate
the hexayurt model to the crowd.

10.Everything You Wanted to Know

About Building a Shantytown, But Did Not Know Who to Ask

COMPOST TOILETS

EARLY IN THE LOGISTICAL discussions with the Lake Worth Kids, the issue of facilities arose. Even if we found a port-a-potty company willing to deliver in the middle of a hostile land takeover, we were by no means assured that we could pay for the toilet, or that we wanted a chemical-based unit, given the environmental commitment of the Kids.

The solution: compost toilets. On the outside, compost toilets look like regular port-a-potties (although they do not have to, any constructed box could do), but the "guts" or disposal system was different.

In the traditional port-a-potty, the disposal system basically consists of a large container filled with chemicals that break down excrement and odors. A truck shows up on occasion to suck out the contents of the container and replenish the chemicals, which are strong but destructive to the environment, particularly when spillage occurs.

Compost toilets on the other hand are buckets or other containers, and composting materials such as sawdust or even dirt. After using the facilities, one simply scoops the compost materials and covers the human waste. The containers are then emptied into a large compost bin on a regular basis. After a year or so of airing out, the contents of the bin can be used as fertilizer. The process is natural, renewable, environmentally sound and economically feasible.

Two days before the takeover, we "liberated" a port-a-potty shell. It was not in use and just filthy inside. The Kids cleaned it like new and removed the chemical container, as well as the vent from the back, facilitating the insert and exit of the bucket.

After no arrests were made on October 23, we delivered the shell and demonstrated proper compost toilet usage and maintenance to the residents and volunteers. Most understood and adhered to the rules, but some simply did not get it and others somehow made it to the toilet before we made it clear to them.

Compost duty—rotating and cleaning full buckets with empty ones—was not the most pleasant task on the land, but probably the most important.

Once we reached about thirty residents—which only took a month—one toilet was not enough, and the thought of more than one compost toilet was unbearable for most, including the neighbors who were forced to endure some unusual odors when inadequate amounts of coverings were used.

Eventually we broke down and ordered one, and then a second, traditional port-a-potty. However, the lessons of composting will stick with many of us.

CONSTRUCTION AND PATRIARCHY

The Umoja construction crew was led by Rebecca, an anarchist living in Miami. She was extremely handy and talented at construction and transferring knowledge to others, which was one of her charges.

With Rebecca in charge of construction, the nature of patriarchy was laid bare for all to see, at least for all who cared to notice.

For the record, I know very little about constructing and building, and during the entire life of the Village, I barely constructed anything at all, even though I sought to understand what was going on for my own body of knowledge. However, time and again, men and women—but mainly men—assumed that I was in charge of construction, even as I was never caught with a hammer. They asked me how the shanties were constructed and I would introduce them to Rebecca, our lead construction person, and she would explain the idea and process.

On multiple occasions, men would look away from Rebecca, who did all the talking, to look me in the eye and ask me a question about what Rebecca was saying. She would then answer the question and they would, again, look at me to ask the follow-up question. It was shocking.

As we expanded construction, my opinion was often sought, and I weighed in on non-technical issues, such as where the next shanty should sit, which direction it should face or what was the best paint color. Much of the time I deferred to Rebecca, who was in charge of construction (did I mention that Rebecca, not me, was in charge of construction?). Still, most men wanted to hear the instructions from me, not from her.

The patriarchal domain men exercised over the area of construction was even more perplexing given the fact that most of the construction, at least in the first few weeks, was not only led but also implemented by women. Lynne, Cara (a Lake Worth, Florida Commissioner), Monique and Madelyn, Poncho, Amanda and so many others were hard at work building shanties while so many men sat around talking about the hard work involved in building the shanties.

One bright spot was one of our early volunteers, Leon Thomas. I had met Thomas years prior, after his brother, Duke Dailey, was shot and killed by North Miami police on Father's Day 2001. Duke was wheelchair-bound and had been shot four times, in the back, as he rolled away from a cop who told him to stop. When he heard about Umoja, Thomas—who is in the construction business—offered his expertise.

In spite of his expertise and considerable work experience, Thomas accepted Rebecca's leadership, making suggestions where he could, while asking permission and opinions on everything from design to bracing and everything else.

Rebecca and the Lake Worth Kids did an amazing job of planning and building, a task which was daunting enough without the constant pull of patriarchy.

PALLET PALACES

The shanties in which people lived were nicknamed the Pallet Palaces. They were constructed of wooden pallets, those used by businesses to store and move inventory. Forklifts are used to lift pallets off the ground or from shelves, and businesses regularly throw them out after shipments and stocking.

As such, the Kids scavenged for pallets all over town, picking up small quantities of pallets near business trash bins. We realized very quickly, however, that our needs were significantly outstripping the supply, and eventually purchased the pallets for $2 a piece.

Each shanty required twenty pallets in all, plus two pieces of 8x10 plywood and some tarp, cardboard and nails. The structures were remarkably simple to build, sturdy and efficient.

The palace backs consisted of two vertical rows of three pallets, forming a wall approximately 6 feet, 5 inches high and 12 feet wide. Each side consisted of two rows of two pallets, creating a depth of about 8 feet. An additional 2x2 pallet wall was installed in the center of each unit, converting each structure into a duplex. Two more pallets were stacked at the entrance, attached to the center wall, as a frame for the door.

Each unit, then, was 8 feet deep and about 6 feet wide. The walls were nailed together and braced at all significant joints, and even some less significant ones.

The roofs required a bit of a rise or pitch, so as to run off rainwater. The two plywood sheets were secured on the top, at a pitch, and covered with a large tarp. The walls were covered with flattened cardboard boxes, which were then painted over with acrylic paint—which, it turns out, is waterproof.

Anything from a blanket to a fully-functional door served the needs of privacy and security. The duplex design not only maximized pallet usage, but also built in accountability among neighbors, as the actions of one directly impacted the quality of life of the other.

SHOWERS AND GARDENS

We needed a shower and, again, Rebecca figured that whole thing out. We found some tiles and laid them on a modest dirt-based elevation to serve as the shower floor.

The walls were constructed of pallets, a traditional shower curtain served as the door and a tin sheet worked as the roof. A five-gallon bucket, painted black to attract the sun, was elevated and placed towards the rear of the shower. A pipe and valve were installed at the bottom of the bucket.

Outside of the shower, a rudimentary ladder was placed to enable the shower taker to climb and pour water into the top of the elevated bucket. After allowing the water to warm up a bit in the sun, one enters the shower and opens the valve, enabling gravity to work its magic.

The cracks between the tiles on the floor were utilitarian. Two pipes were placed under the elevated tiles, capturing the run-off water, delivering it to the adjacent garden bed. Every shower not only cleaned a resident, but helped grow collard greens and other vegetables.

NAMING UMOJA

Less than a week after the takeover, I had sat for a rare spell at home, scribbling furiously in my notebook, brainstorming. Bernadette inquired, so I told her about the half-dozen or so things I was working on, including coming up with proposed names for the Village.

She listened to my list of names, which I had been working on since before the takeover, and was thoroughly unimpressed. "Why don't you name it 'Umoja' for unity?"

I literally rolled my eyes and audibly scoffed. "It's Swahili, another language, people are not going to be into it. Forget it." I wanted to nip her sudden helpfulness in the bud, because she tends to jump in during the middle of a project, making suggestions with a smug attitude of righteousness.

It didn't work.

"Why not? The residents are all about the unity, you're a Pan-African, it makes total sense. Try it, people will be into it." I tried for several minutes to convince her that I already "knew" the residents, their collective likes, dislikes and tastes, and they would not like "Umoja" for unity, but she persisted until I agreed to include the word on the list of proposed names, in exchange for some peace and quiet.

A few days later, several residents talked on the living room couches and I brought up the subject. Everyone was excited about naming the shantytown and we jumped right into the list of a dozen or so suggestions. The list was quickly narrowed in half and then down to the final four.

I scanned the list and "Umoja" was on it.

At this point, the concept of promoting self-determination did not seem nearly as important as avoiding a lifetime of Bernadette holding this "victory," if we can all it that, over my head. "That shirt does look great on you. Remember how I was right about 'Umoja'?" My heartbeat quickened and I contemplated the ethics of unduly influencing the resident process of naming the shantytown.

When the list was down to the final two, I knew I was cooked. By the time the group selected "Umoja Village" for real, I was already thinking of ways to avoid the conversation with her altogether. I wondered what the chances were that she forgot about the naming ceremony taking place later that same week.

When I got home, I was unusually quiet.

"How is the village?" she asked, as usual.

"Fine. Same thing. We are building. A few new residents. Mostly uneventful. How about your day?" I ventured, hoping to change the subject.

"Okay. So what did they decide?"

"Um. Who?"

"You know, the residents. For the naming ceremony this week. What is the name of the shantytown?"

"Oh, it's not important. It's a shantytown, we can just call it the shantytown."

She saddled up to me grinning from ear to ear, deliberately, and oh-so-cruelly, placing both arms around me.

"So," she said, leaning in close to my face. "I was right..."

SELF-DETERMINATION

A core component of our model involved the self-determination of the black community in general and the residents in particular. The residents, therefore, not only ran their affairs in relation to the broader powers-that-be, but also ran their affairs in relation to us, the organizers.

This concept was made real in many forms. For example, the Lake Worth Kids and others were required not only to build the initial units of housing, but also to train the residents on how to build the units themselves, ultimately making the residents self-reliant in matters of building and repair. At some point, the organizers would, as a general rule, not pick up trash on the land, as the residents were to exercise both rights and responsibilities on their land.

While I was most closely associated with Umoja, Poncho took the ultimate step and essentially moved into the Village herself. She lived in a shanty, organized volunteers and dealt with ongoing issues twenty-four hours a day, seven days a week. Part of her job was to pass on her skill set and experience to the residents so that they could run the Village themselves, a plan that met with success.

The primary means of exercising self-determination, however, took the form of Sunday Meetings. Each and every Sunday at 5:00PM, we met in the living room to discuss all matters Umoja, large and small. We talked about supplies, use of the kitchen, late night security detail, arguments on the land, trash cleanup, the latest threats on Umoja and everything in between.

During Sunday meetings, residents aired grievances and looked to resolve conflicts. When two residents argued bitterly during the week, instead of taking it off the land, they took it to Sunday Meeting. We listened to both sides and suggested, even mandated, potential remedies to each situation.

Residents voted to stop or resume building units, the rules of the land, who had to leave and who was moving in.

There were a number of occasions during which residents were asked to leave, either for a few days or for good. A few were voted off for multiple violations of taking food from the kitchen, but most were voted off for being a consistent nuisance and breaking the peace. Particularly in the beginning, most of those removed were assumed to have been sent by someone intent upon triggering behavior to justify a raid on the land.

The debate was always passionate and it was every resident's responsibility to enforce decisions made. It was empowering to witness poor black people respecting each other—and themselves—enough to make and enforce their own rules, rather than asking the state to intervene. The process proved we are fully capable of handling our own affairs without the intervention of the police.

The difficulty lay in determining the points at which the organizers should lead, intervene or just facilitate the discussion and decision making. At times we intervened too much, robbing the residents of their right to make their own decisions, including their own mistakes, and at times we erred on the opposite end of the spectrum, failing to provide the required amount of political leadership.

At some point, the residents began to assert their right to even greater autonomy in their decision making. The sentiment arose after one or more of the organizers second-guessed resident decisions, and informally worked toward a reconsideration. This happened mainly after a resident was suspended or expelled from the land and one of the organizers felt sorry for the newly departed.

Such interventions, however, created a dynamic in which an offender essentially had two chances at redemption—first by pleading their case to the residents during Sunday meeting, and then by appealing to the organizers. While the organizers acted in compassion, the end result undermined the self-determination of the residents. As such, the residents asserted their right to self-determination.

It was a terribly exciting time, watching residents graduate from no power at all to a recognition that significant power is not enough.

The road ahead was not easy, as residents learned how to wield power. Sometimes they did not use it often or quickly enough, while other times they were too swift and too harsh in meting out justice.

Come to think of it, those are some of the same mistakes made by all others in power.

Liberation is not a destination, it is a journey.

Ministers side with the government and
call for the destruction of Umoja.

Police move supporters off the land.

Paris Brouard defends the land.
(Photo courtesy of Cindy Karp)

10. Six-Month Anniversary

KEEPING THE UMOJA VILLAGE up and running was at times turbulent, but an always rewarding challenge. The challenges kept coming, but at some point, the Village itself stabilized as a result of a confluence of factors.

STOPPING THE ATTACKS

The first factor was that after the initial series of attempts to shut down the Village, the attacks subsided significantly.

The Super Bowl was scheduled to be played in Miami early in 2007. As a media spectacle, local government officials had no interest in having people think Miami was anything other than a tropical paradise with no corruption or housing crisis whatsoever. We were not surprised, then, to hear rumors through the grapevine that city and county officials were plotting to raze the Village.

Miami City Commissioner Michelle Spence-Jones, in whose district the Umoja Village rose, proposed an ordinance accomplishing two things:

first, it mandated anyone engaged in an "assembly" on "exempt public property," must first obtain a permit from the police department. Second, the ordinance re-classified vacant lots as "exempt public property."

The ordinance was an obvious attempt to circumvent the Pottinger Settlement, Umoja's legal protection, by redefining the Village as an assembly rather than what it was—homeless people living on vacant public land. The attempt surely would have failed legal challenge, but the goal was to get us off the land and shut down the Village before the media covering the Super Bowl rolled into town, even if the law was struck down later in court. And like so many attempts to limit our rights, the ordinance induced all kinds of presumably unintended consequences.

Technically, the ordinance outlawed two people cutting through an empty field as a shortcut to the store, school or a friend's house, unless the people, a week or so prior to the journey, applied for a police permit to "assemble" across the field, and were approved.

However, by defining the applicable areas as "exempt public property," vacant lots joined other such properties, including libraries, police stations, city hall and hospitals. Consequently, if the ordinance passed, anyone "assembled" at city hall to petition the government, or a hospital to visit a loved one—without pre-approval from the police—was, technically, in violation of the law. So was, incidentally, an "assembly" to the police station to report a violation of the assembly law. The ordinance was absurd and we relished the opportunity to compel the police to enforce the new law. We planned to visit hospitals and libraries, dialing 911 to report the "crimes" we witnessed, demanding immediate arrests. On video tape, of course.

More importantly for our purposes, the passage of the law would set the stage for a police raid, arresting residents and activists for engaging in an illegal assembly, dismantling the shanties in the process.

The backlash against the ordinance was immediate and vicious. Ministers, already scheduled for a generic "hands off Umoja Village" press event, ripped into Spence-Jones and the city. None was harsher than Rev. Richard Dunn, who reamed Spence-Jones so harshly, some residents pitied her. At the time, Dunn was Spence-Jones's mortal enemy, having lost a bitter election to her. Months later, however, Dunn and Spence-Jones would bury the hatchet and come together in calling for the end of Umoja.

The media took its turn and slammed Spence-Jones, particularly in the context of the broader housing crisis. It was also revealed her family recently accepted a $75,000 grant from the county to start a business, making her attempts to evict homeless people making no demands on government money whatsoever appear heartless. The black press was particularly sharp in their critique. Individuals, organizations and impacted groups responded with calls, e-mails, faxes and statements of support.

Most surprisingly, a sitting elected official, City of Miami Commissioner Tomas Regalado, came to Umoja and donated clothes and food before announcing that if the Commission passed the ordinance, he would walk off the dais, drive to the shantytown and the police would have to arrest him first for violating the new law. It was profound that the only elected official to stand shoulder to shoulder with us was a right leaning white Cuban male, a fact which speaks poorly of the scoundrels who weasel their way into elected office in the name of the black community.

In Miami, ordinances become effective only after passing two votes or "readings." After passing on first reading, Spence-Jones pulled the ordinance before the second and final reading. At the end of the process, we emerged stronger and more stable, giving notice that we would not go down without a fight.

CONSOLIDATING OUR SUPPORT

The second factor contributing to our stability was the consolidation of our support. After getting over the initial shock of our taking land, individuals and organizations put their full support behind us. A constant stream of volunteers and donations rolled in, contributions without which we could not have survived.

Our rotation of organizers and volunteers also stabilized. Myself, Amanda and General Rashid continued to put in long hours, but they were regular long hours not 24/7 long hours. Poncho, who had essentially moved into and managed the Village for several months, suffered the inevitable burnout of the job and moved back home. This was a great loss, but fortunately, a host of other volunteers stepped up and provided support, including Linda Sippio, Rebecca, Jewel Parham and others.

The biggest leap in this area, however, arrived in the form of Mamyrah Prosper. After hearing about the Village, Mamyrah called me a few times, but I was too busy to respond properly. Eventually, I invited her to a presentation I made at the Human Services Coalition where I could present to the group and her at the same time, avoiding repetition. As it turned out, a city flunky showed up and he and I engaged in a shouting match, allowing Mamyrah the opportunity to see exactly what she was getting into. I am not sure if she was undeterred or encouraged by the exchange, but she signed up to volunteer.

Mamyrah stepped in and up, contributing immediately. She worked hard, was reliable and consistently principled in her approach to our dilemmas and decision making. I admired her willingness, even eagerness, to challenge difficult situations head-on. Her potential was clearly recognizable and it was not long before she was an integral and irreplaceable part of the team. Remember the name Mamyrah Prosper, as her leadership potential is great and you will be hearing about her for quite some time.

THE RESIDENTS TAKE OVER

The final factor in stabilizing Village life was the collective decision of the residents to demand greater power from the organizers. While residents made decisions and rules during Sunday Meetings, they remained dependent upon the organizers to run the meetings, for organizing resources and projects and for our role as arbiters and peacemakers.

When disputes arose, as they do anytime fifty people live together in tight quarters, and they were unable to work things out themselves, residents called on one of the organizers to mediate or "approve" a settlement, as residents learned to run their own city and relate to one another in a new society. In another sense, residents lacked the confidence in their own decision making abilities, which they had rarely enjoyed the opportunity to exercise on that level prior to Umoja.

The results of the organizer intervention were mixed. The organizers influenced positively by offering alternate models of problem solving, and political paradigms from which the residents could evaluate situations and make decisions. On the other hand, at some point, residents became overly dependent upon the organizers to resolve conflicts they were more than qualified to resolve themselves. Some residents recognized this quagmire and took full advantage.

One resident, for example, was voted off the land, on the spot, by the other residents for serious and repeated transgressions of the rules. He immediately appealed to one of the organizers, who had no direct knowledge of the severity of the multiple infractions. Feeling sympathetic, the organizer returned to the land and used their moral authority to plead for a second chance, which at this point was a twentieth or thirtieth chance.

The residents' trust in us ultimately led to the overturning of the vote. However, the process, which was well intentioned, unintentionally undermined the authority of the residents, deflating their confidence.

After discussing the item privately, residents organized themselves and raised the subject during Sunday Meeting. The residents demanded their decisions remain final, with no interference from the organizers. In addition, while they still wanted our general help, they demanded a transfer of responsibilities directly to the residents. We proudly agreed.

Residents Jungle Queen and Jugg both stepped up to fill the leadership and management void. They each were given keys to the kitchen and storage room, which meant both elements were in the full control of the residents—no organizer had a copy. The two essentially managed the Village for the remainder of its existence.

It was a difficult task, enforcing the rules and determining the humane circumstances under which the rules were to be bent, and they did a marvelous job. I venture to say that in another setting, Jungle Queen and Jugg could professionally manage any sized company, outshining most top managers.

When tough decisions were made or incidents arose, the residents kept me informed, but I was careful to limit my comments unless I was specifically asked or there were some clearly harmful decisions being made.

As difficult as it was to watch the residents make mistakes, two things kept me in check. First: knowing that we, the organizers, made mistakes as well. There is something fundamentally unfair about allowing one group to make mistakes while denying that right to another. And secondly: I internalized the words of Kwame Nkrumah, the first President of the liberated Ghana, when he said it was preferable to live in self-rule and chaos than to live in subjugation and tranquility. Part of freedom includes the freedom to make mistakes, and there is nothing unique about a group making mistakes.

Overall, the road was rough, particularly as the residents grappled with their power to kick people off the land and wielding that power fairly and compassionately. As they exercised self-determination, the residents increasingly took ownership over the Umoja Village.

THE NEXT GENERATION SHANTYTOWN

We discussed the realities, challenges and new developments on an ongoing basis, constantly assessing our needs and shortcomings while confronting our external challenges, mitigating them and utilizing them as teachable moments for the residents and ourselves.

Our assessments were brutally honest, not because we were cruel or enjoyed reviewing our failures in agonizing detail, but because our assessments determined our actions and the future direction of the entire project. Our people deserve appropriate solutions to real problems. Those problems can only be analyzed and solved via a thorough process of meaningful and rigorous reflection. Anything less is a disservice to our people. Anything less for the purpose of sparing one's feelings is vanity.

In any event, our assessments led to a plan to advance the Umoja Village to the next level. We developed four actionable areas: deepen our roots on the land; expand our political reach beyond the land; provide resident services; and promote resident development.

Given the extent to which we had consolidated our support and grown into a community institution, we felt that we could simultaneously deepen our roots on and expand our political reach beyond the land.

Deepening our roots meant ensuring the Village remained over the long term. We devised several strategies to do that, including dealing with the newly created Housing Task Force formed by Commissioner Spence-Jones as a kinder, gentler way of getting us off the land; getting a mailbox to establish permanent residency for the residents; digging a well for drinking water; and, most visibly, building the next generation shanties.

We researched options to make the shanties more comfortable and better looking and to provide better protection against the elements. Summer was coming and we did not look forward to enduring the Miami heat in wood boxes. After summer comes hurricane season, which could force us to take down the entire village, store it and rebuild it from scratch again—every time a hurricane approached Miami.

Rebecca eventually found our solution: the hexayurt. Hexayurts were designed as easily built and broken down refugee shelters, providing basic shelter from the elements. It was a great concept and we were excited about being the first settlement to employ hexayurts for mass use.

Anyone interested in the idea should research the hexayurt themselves. The units are built to last twenty years and because they are made out of insulation they provide protection against the heat, are easily collapsible—an obvious advantage during hurricane season—and are fire retardant.

We built a small model on the land and the residents laughed out loud, calling them "space ships." I knew we would encounter some resistance, but we all understood that the existing shanties were not long term solutions, and I was confident that once the first few units were built, the residents would line up for them. We scheduled the construction of the first hexayurt for 10:00AM on April 26, 2007, three days after our six-month anniversary celebration.

As a means of expanding our political reach beyond the land, we resolved to invest our political capital on the broader issues of land, gentrification and housing. After spending the majority of our time and energy simply defending our position on the land, the fight paid off with solid community support and a layer of political and legal protection around us, making eviction attempts politically difficult.

We devised several new campaigns and took positions on the campaigns advocated by other organizations, planning to step out and engage in the broader political discourse.

In spite of their pride, dignity and demands for greater power over their lives, our residents endured many of the social ills plaguing other poor and homeless populations. In response, we moved to make quality social services available to residents.

As our situation stabilized and the threats against us diminished, we were free to pursue social services for the residents—such as job training, jobs, drug treatment, public assistance to which they were entitled, continued education and more.

We were determined to overwhelm the residents with social services by forcing the corresponding agencies to do their jobs and provide services to their client population. Providing those services ourselves was not only outside of our political model, but would drain our resources at a time when agencies proclaimed to the media that they could help all of the Umoja residents if only given the opportunity.

With respect to permanent housing, some agencies housed a few of our residents, but because the need is so great, the shanties were quickly refilled. It did not take long for those agencies to recognize that if people were left with the impression that the best way to get housing was to spend a few days or weeks at Umoja, our wait list would soon number in the thousands, creating an interest for even a greater number of people to defend our existence and success.

Finally, because running the village required constant response to emergencies, we had failed in providing clear and consistent political orientation and spaces for formal political education for the residents, a failure we resolved to correct with resident development.

Initially, we conducted weekly political education sessions, during which we discussed important political issues, such as land struggles, gentrification, capitalism, patriarchy, white supremacy and more. When the concerted efforts to remove us from the land began, the political education sessions were the easiest item to drop from the agenda. Consequently, the political context of the shantytown was discussed in general terms, but not in a consistent and organized manner.

This failing only grew in importance as our first round of residents graduated to permanent housing and the new residents arrived without experiencing formal political education. We failed to build a common understanding among new arrivals of our political mission, beyond what they absorbed during our media tours or special events. It was a disservice to the residents and to the movement.

As such, we would reconstitute the political education and leadership development aspects of the Umoja Village, ensuring residents understood what we were doing in a broad political way, not just as an alternative to the shelter.

We discussed our ideas with the residents, and announced our ambitious program during our six-month anniversary celebration on April 23, 2007. It was an empowering moment, which energized our residents and supporters. If the first six months were good, the next six months would be great.

Umoja Village after the fire.

Residents sift through rubble
looking for personal effects.

Breakfast in the parking lot.

11. The Fire

MY PHONE RANG AT about 12:30 on Thursday morning. I had been asleep for less than an hour, and suddenly realized the ringing was not a dream.

Jugg was on the other line screaming. "Max, shantytown is burned down, man." I told him to calm down and tell me what happened. He managed to repeat the claim, talking about a fire and trucks and people running. I told him I would be right there and hung up to get dressed.

Perhaps because it had been months since the last time I received a late-night call requesting my return to the land to problem solve, the words "burned down" and "fire" simply did not register in my mind they way they should have. As I rose to get dressed, it never occurred to me that the Village might really have burned down.

Before I had a chance to get dressed and tell Bernadette what the commotion was about, the phone rang again, this time with local activist Altine Baki on the other end. "The shantytown's on fire, bro! Get down here!" Before I could respond to her, the other line was ringing with a similar message.

Having just completed a three day fast, I grabbed some fruits to eat in the car and sped off. During the short ride from my home to the Village, I starting thinking about what was going on there. I was only a few blocks from home when the phone rang again. I'm not sure why it took so long, but as I hung up on this fourth call in ten minutes, for the first time I thought the unthinkable: "could the shantytown have burned down?"

It was surprisingly difficult to imagine the Village completely burned to the ground, so I thought about sections being gone and parts burned down, and how we would go about the business of repairing those units.

Rolling up 62nd Street, numerous police cars were in sight, two at the 15th Avenue intersection, at least four more in view and even more around the corner. I realized that Jugg was not exaggerating. I parked on 15th Avenue and looked up 62nd Terrace, the street framing the Village on the North side. The fire truck stood with its fully-extended ladder reaching into the night sky, the hose oscillating back and forth dousing water downward on what would be the rear portion of the Village.

My mind raced to recall all of the people who might have trouble running and getting out of a difficult situation—Mr. Cata, Mr. Fredrick, Roosevelt, Lanish, Micah, Gypsy Bird, Jungle Queen. Any of them could get trapped in their room, cut off by flames and the commotion.

The police would not allow me onto 62nd Terrace, so I jogged up 62nd Street and saw residents congregating in the parking lot of the bar across the street from the land. People were shocked, upset and distraught. They endured the same range of emotions as anyone losing their home to a fire, hurricane or other sudden disaster. I hugged each resident as I saw them; some cried; some were shocked into stiffness and non-responsive.

I asked about each resident, we took a head count and accounted for every soul. Not only did everyone make it out alive, we had only one minor injury, sustained by Jugg, who hurt his ankle as he heroically carried a sleeping Mr. Roosevelt out of his room and into safety. Clayton, one of our neighbors in the apartment next door, did the same, clearing one shanty after the next and carrying Lanish over his shoulders to the parking lot across the street.

The heroism and compassion—dare I say love—displayed by our residents and neighbors for each other was heartwarming. Their actions during and after the fire epitomized the sense of community we had sought to build. Two people walked into structures made of wood and cardboard while those structures were (or were about to be) ablaze, in order to save other people they knew only by sharing a vacant lot with them. Is there a way to teach compassion and heroics? I don't have the answer to that, but I do know that we built something together, and what we built was evident in the early hours of April 26, 2007.

"I HAVE GREAT NEWS"

As the fire trucks pulled out, we came together in the bar parking lot to discuss and decide. While most were in the parking lot on the south side of the land, others were on 62nd Terrace to the north, so we waited on them to arrive.

Organizers and supporters started to show up, roused from their sleep by our informal communications network, a network which, apparently, had yet to learn not to call people in the middle of the night. I updated Bernadette and she called Julia Daniel, a strong supporter and member of Power U. Julia agreed to come to our home and stay with our son, Akinle, for the rest of the morning so that Bernadette could come to the land.

People were still shocked, some quiet, some sobbing, some angry and probably more than a few in denial. I did not realize it at the time, but I was in denial myself.

Just to put this in context, most residents lost everything they owned. They lost food, which might not seem like a big deal to people who eat on a daily basis, but for our residents, it was a significant loss. Clothes, including "professional" and church gear, certificates of achievement, identification, legal documents, family photos and other one-of-a-kind family heirlooms. There are no insurance forms to fill out nor a big check on the horizon.

For a number of people, contained in the Village was everything they had accumulated in this phase of their lives and, suddenly, those belongings were gone. There is no way to over play the significance of the loss.

In addition, the residents lost their community. They lost something which was a great source of pride, and for a growing number, an important part of their identity. Previous to their arrival, most residents were ignored and disrespected, suffering under the social stigma of homelessness, racism and classism. At Umoja, however, students, activists and the news media came to see and recognize them.

What do you say to people who lost everything in life, then recently regained a sense dignity and hope in an unlikely setting, and then lost it all over again in a sudden, tragic fire? What do you say to people who volunteered hours of their lives to build a place—more than a place—that is now a pile of charcoal and rubble? They gathered, some with soot on their faces and clothes, some with no shoes or socks on their feet and all with pain and confusion on their faces.

As the circle slowly took shape in the parking lot of a bar, it was eerily quiet and desperate eyes peered at me from every direction. Are they searching for answers, or detailed instructions or comfort or inspiration? What is there to say to people who lost all of their material possessions? The answer came easily.

"I have great news," I exclaimed. "After this devastating fire, I am happy to announce that we do not have one single casualty or injury!"

People looked at each other, smiled, clapped and hugged. The mood palpably altered upwards as some smiled for the first time since the fire and the residents began interacting with one another normally again.

We struck a collective epiphany: the fire was tragic and we lost a great many material things, however, in this Village, in this new society, wood structures, clothing, radios and other things we collected are not what is important. Important to us are the human beings and the quality of their lives.

In the end, we can get new donations, replace radios and bedding, purchase more food. But we cannot replace human beings, our lovers, our neighbors, our friends, or our sisters and brothers.

One of our political objectives in taking back the land was building a new society, one in which people were valued over profits and material things. Throughout the existence of the Umoja Village, we wrung our hands and gnashed our teeth over the thought that we had not done enough to root this ideal in our portion of the world.

As the firefighters gave the all clear for us to return to the portion of the land which was unimpacted by the fire, we embarked upon the long trek across the four lanes of NW 62nd Street, four familiar lanes, which suddenly seemed unbearably long and simultaneously leading us home and to an unfamiliar and uncharted destination.

En masse, we crossed the road, indistinguishable from the millions of this planet's refugees trekking from one part of the world to another, hungry, tired and beaten, yet at the same time somehow prideful and determined in a quest to recapture that elusive dream: our land.

As I watched the two dozen or so human forms—some coupled, some singular—journey across the street, in the dark stillness that is two o'clock in the morning, I mused over our quest to build a new society, and the notion that we might have advanced our mission a bit further than we initially suspected.

That night, we fed the remaining residents—the ones who did not take the van to the homeless shelter—and prepared sleeping areas on the portion of the land not impacted by the fire. I walked down to 15th Avenue to retrieve my car and then parked on the land. I walked around our new encampment to count the residents and ensure that everything was well. I prioritized our tasks for the morning and then took one more look at the devastation, eager to begin the rebuilding process. The prospect of building bigger and better than before was exciting and I relished the opportunity.

At about 4:00AM, I retired to my car, reclined my seat and fell asleep. Not long after, a splash of sun woke me and, for a brief moment, I was disoriented, wondering why I was in my car at the break of day. I sat up, peered out of the car window and achieved instant and total recall...

Bernadette and I try to figure things out.

Police arrest Amanda for causing "an affray." All charges are later dropped.

After Tony Romano of the Miami Workers Center, I am arrested.

13. Umoja Rising

The day after the fire, it was still shocking and offensive to drive by the land and see it trapped and contained by a barbed wire fence. April 26 lasted twenty-four hours, like any other day, but the whirlwind of events and roller coaster of emotions provided a lifetime's worth of excitement, drama and disappointment. We lost our housing; we regained our humanity; we were forced off the land; the community came together to make a heroic stand and we were arrested, moved off and fenced out.

We were left physically and emotionally drained and, with several residents at the Homeless Assistance Center, numerically depleted. Still, we were ready to fight for the land.

Even with the will to fight, the truth was that our power was significantly diminished by the fact that we were off of the land. Our leverage and power emanated from our physical occupation of the land, with the residents prepared to fight for their homes and supporters willing to help. After the fire and our eviction from the land, we were no longer fighting to hold our ground, we were now fighting to get back on the land, a different proposition entirely. We lost the strategic and psychological advantage we had enjoyed while in control of Umoja and the land upon which it sat.

I recalled our first day on the land and the empowering psychological impact of watching the police driving off the lot, leaving the land to the community. Standing with residents and neighbors outside of the fence looking in, I felt an inverse and proportionate impact of dis-empowerment and even defeat. Regaining control over the land, then, was critical to the psyche of our community and the movement.

We gathered the troops, including residents, the Lake Worth Kids and other supporters, to assess our emotional state, and everyone was ready and anxious to fight for the land. Having tasted liberation and self-determination and running their own affairs, the transition back to the streets for the residents was brutal and almost unbearable. Their sentiments towards the land only deepened as they spent more time off the land and under the bridges or park benches.

We recommitted ourselves to the notion that the black community must control the land—all of it—in our community, and resist the temptation to reduce the struggle to a single piece of real estate. Therefore, whether or not our attempts to re-take Umoja was successful, ultimately, we would liberate other land.

In pursuit of our objective, we planned a week of action from Monday extending through Friday. We targeted the land and several other vacant, publicly-owned lots in Liberty City, Little Haiti and Overtown. Our informal network reached out and secured commitments from numerous supporters, over a dozen of whom agreed to participate in arrest actions.

After making banners, flyers and other visual props, we planned to spend the latter part of the weekend engaging the community in a door to door campaign to raise awareness and build support for our actions.

On Monday, we planned to retake the land, even if temporarily, by cutting through the fence engaging in arrest actions. We planned to erect instant shantytowns on several lots around town, including in Overtown, close to downtown. In addition, the Miami Corporate Run, an annual event in which upwards of 30,000 people—mostly through the large corporations which employ them—participate in a 5k run/walk through downtown, was scheduled during our week of action. We planned to erect a shanty in the middle of the race.

We planned four arrest actions over five days, followed by a weekend erecting shanties all over the City of Miami. When the powers attack a people's movement, they only back off or change positions when the negative consequences of their actions are greater than the gains. Our mission, then, was to force the city to pay for the land they wanted so badly. The political consequences of our week of action would raise the price of the land and the city would have to decide if they were willing to pay such a price.

A MUTUAL FRIEND

As the finishing touches were added to the plan, a good friend came to inform me that District 5 Commissioner Michelle Spence-Jones wanted to meet one-on-one to discuss granting the land to a group selected by Umoja in order to construct low-income housing. While the idea was intriguing, there was no way I was going to meet with Spence-Jones, about this subject without any witnesses.

I brought the news to the larger group and, after some initial confliction, the consensus was that we should listen to the proposal and then decide, collectively, whether to accept the offer. We established objectives and parameters for the talks, such as securing two lots of land, one for construction and the other for building a shantytown until construction was complete; cash to assist with the development; and that the city house our residents until the construction completed. Most importantly, if the offer was insincere, we were under no obligation to play nice, and were encouraged to express our indignation and walk out of the meeting.

Armed with our parameters, Umoja resident John Cata accompanied me to Spence-Jones's place of business for the talks. When she offered the land we immediately countered that one lot was insufficient. Anticipating our demands, she was prepared to offer us the vacant lot that sat across 17th Avenue and assured us staff was busy looking into available cash to help with startup costs. Cata and I demanded the city provide housing for each and every one of our residents in need and she agreed.

Spence-Jones explained that she was looking for commercial space on the ground floor and residential units on the top. In addition, she said in order for the deal to fly, we would have to partner with a reputable developer, suggesting Carrfour Supportive Housing, a not-for-profit with a strong track record of developing low-income supportive housing for the homeless and formerly homeless.

What Spence-Jones did not know is that Carrfour had contacted us months prior asking to partner with us to build on the land. In preparation for our six month anniversary, we started, but never consummated, talks with Carrfour regarding the development of supportive housing on the land, including ground floor commercial. As such, by agreeing to Spence-Jones's terms, we made no concessions as we were already in the early stages of developing a virtually identical proposal.

We explained that we had to bring the offer back to the group, but we had more pressing issues on our mind. What we really wanted to know was when they were taking down the fence? Our people needed somewhere to stay and we were anxious to get back on the land and start building our hexayurts. The real reason we were there, and what everyone in the larger group was eager to learn, was to find out when were we re-establishing the Umoja Village?

She looked at me like I done lost my mind.

"There is no more shantytown. You cannot build anymore shanties. We are giving you the land, you cannot build any shanties!"

After several minutes of back and forth, if finally dawned on me that this was the deal. The shantytown was nothing but a headache and a black eye for the city, and, consequently, giving away some land and cash in exchange for folding the Village was a great trade for them. I'm a bit embarrassed to admit that I never saw that deal coming, and probably speaks to the extent to which I was still in denial about the loss we suffered.

The thought struck me again and yet, seemingly for the very first time: the Umoja Village is gone. And now the city is offering us the land, but not the Village that sat on the land.

While some think parting ways with wooden shanties is a good thing, part of what forged the strong bond between the residents and their village was the fact that they built and maintained the village themselves. They did not move into a completed home or a community in which they had no power. They loved their community because they built Umoja themselves. Home was not a destination, it was a symbiotic process, which impacted the resident and the community proportionately.

As I mulled over the offer, and its implications, over and again I wondered if we could ever recapture the magic and power of Umoja inside of concrete walls, built by hired hands. Perhaps the reason residents and supporters loved Umoja so much was because they built it, employing a labor of love and belief in something larger than ourselves. I am certain that sense of ownership and pride could not be duplicated in the context of industrial construction. I could not help but to wonder if in trading up to standard housing, we would be giving up the intangibles that had transformed Umoja from a series of wooden boxes into homes and a community.

NATURAL CONCLUSIONS AND THE NATURE OF VICTORY

We pulled together our core supporters to discuss the offer, even as everyone understood that the black leadership and residents would make the final decision. We engaged in heavy soul searching as we tried to reconnect with our fundamental goals and objectives in the face of this dramatic turn of events.

As a starting point, there was unanimous clarity around the fact that we were not, and have no interest in becoming, developers. While we believed it was important to build housing, it was also important to build and maintain a movement. We had to determine what Take Back the Land, fundamentally, was about—developing housing or building a movement. We willingly sacrificed our time and energy to this project because of our roles in the broader social justice movement. However, once the project transformed or evolved from one of resistance to one of development, it was a different ball game, and not all of us wanted to play that game.

Consequently, while all of us supported the end result—new low-income housing—many wanted to continue their life's work of resistance and movement building, and, therefore, would move on to other progressive projects as the development phase took hold. I was one of them.

Others took it a step further, arguing that Take Back the Land itself, not just the individuals who support it, is fundamentally an opposition movement and, therefore, should not be in the development game at all. They argued we should immediately proceed with another adversarial takeover of land, solidifying and building on our model. The debate raged, but was respectful and healthy, continuing over several weeks.

The debate centered around the "natural conclusion" of a land takeover campaign, and frequently referred to South African and Brazilian land struggles. In most instances, that we knew of anyway, the "natural conclusion" to the land struggle was winning title to the land, even if that title did not translate into a multi-million dollar development.

Most agreed that accepting the land deal did not violate any of our fundamental political objectives of 1) housing and feeding people; 2) asserting the right of the black community to control land in our community; and 3) building a new society. In fact, in some ways, it made those objectives even more achievable, particularly over the long term.

The debate was further complicated by the social and political context under which we would be making our decision. Given the real questions our struggle raised about land "ownership" in the U.S. and the state of our movement, it was not clear that acquiring title, in this setting, necessarily meant the same thing as acquiring title in another social and political setting. That is to say, there are significant differences between indigenous peoples re-claiming their own vacant rural land to build something within their own capacity, and the children of immigrants—both voluntary and forced-—winning an urban lot in an industrial society, with all of the rules and regulations implied therein, from what is essentially land stolen from the Native Americans.

We also debated the impact of the radical shift in demeanor—from a strong oppositional force to engaging with the government—required by our own shift in status from occupier of land to developer. Agreeing to the deal meant shifting from occupying one of the most progressive positions in the land struggle movement, to becoming a developer (ugh!). The monumental shift from opposing corrupt government officials and practices to working with those same corrupt officials to build something together was far too much for some of us to stomach.

We also discussed the "nature of victory," and the fine line, at least in this context, which differentiates victory from selling out. We tried to determine what constituted victory, what constituted selling out to the state and how to delineate the difference in a manner that made sense to us all.

The debate brought two movement tendencies to the surface. First: as the opposition, it is difficult for us to accept victory, even when we win. Virtually any settlement between us and our political targets can be interpreted as a sell-out simply because there is an agreement or because those in power no longer stand against the demand. Consequently, we as a movement must clearly define what constitutes victory, particularly in the context of the U.S. political and economic system.

The second, and related, tendency is to want, in a political settlement, to ensure that the system wins nothing at all. Given our lack of power, this is an understandable tendency, but an impossible proposition. We nearly declined the deal explicitly to prevent officials from pimping our work for their own benefit. Specifically, we knew the same officials responsible for the bad public policy and the squandering of housing funds which facilitated the crisis of gentrification and housing, and actively tried to shut down the Umoja Village, would later use the success of our development to demonstrate how they were addressing the crisis ("The government is building more housing!"). It was infuriating just to think about.

In the end, however, we could not deprive our people of housing just so that we could also deprive crooked officials a propaganda tool, particularly because their propaganda machine is so effective, that they can claim victory regardless of what actually happens. When they win, they win, but even on those occasions when we win and they lose, the propaganda machine finds a way of taking credit for that loss and turning it into a victory.

We also contemplated political realities. If we refused the deal, what message were we sending, in practical and perceived terms, to our residents? We want you to live in boxes, even given the opportunity to significantly upgrade? How would the residents feel (answer: they wanted the freedom of Umoja and the quality of housing built to code, just like other people enjoyed) and how would our supporters react?

During one meeting Lynne, who was unable to attend, submitted a letter expressing her recognition that this was "not my movement," a nod to the black political leadership and the residents, but thoughtfully and principally argued her points. Her letter was as much proof as her work that this was, indeed, her movement as well.

In the end, the majority agreed the land deal was, in fact, a natural conclusion to and a victory for the campaign. Therefore, we would accept the deal. In good faith, those who still believed we should reject the deal and take over more land did not block the settlement, which, essentially, called for a cease-fire.

The legitimate concerns about the deal compromising Take Back the Land's adversarial and oppositional posture, as well as our ability to forge forward with hard core campaigns, would be mitigated by giving the land to Serve the People, Inc., a new 501(c)3, a separate organization, only loosely affiliated with Take Back the Land—but able, as part of its mission, to engage in constructive projects, such as development.

Therefore, a friendly entity would control the land and Take Back the Land could remain entirely oppositional and be ready to resume our core mission.

UMOJA RISING

That Monday afternoon, instead of protests and arrests, we announced the political settlement. The residents and neighbors were very emotional. We made certain all understood that construction would take years and we still had to complete a proposal, and then it must be passed by the City Commission.

Consequently, Take Back the Land, as an organization, faced three major tasks: first, to build a viable post-Umoja organization. Second, to serve the needs of our residents. And third, to figure out how to develop the land.

In pursuit of our post-Umoja organization, Mamyrah, Amanda and I engaged in a process of discussing organizational structure and theory and the role of members and supporters, and engaged in structured study to build political unity, laying the groundwork for building Take Back the Land beyond the Umoja Village.

Serving the residents, however, was the major task that consumed most of our time and energy. In order to keep in touch with residents, track their progress and provide some level of stability in their lives, we re-established the beloved Sunday Meetings a few blocks from the Village at the Brothers of the Same Mind office. Residents came by, broke bread together and remained in contact with us and each other.

Based on her agreement to house the Umoja residents until the new building was completed, Spence-Jones handed off the duty of housing them to the Liberty City Trust, an arm of the city, whose staff are not social workers and exercised dubious commitment and competence in the task.

After the fire, the Trust did step up and house over a dozen of our residents in hotels. However, the residents were clearly selected based on their willingness to hear and dish out gossip about the Umoja Village, not solely on their need for housing. While we were happy the residents found housing, the Trust used the services as a means of sowing the seeds of dissent among a tightly-woven group.

While the Trust played some of the residents, some residents played the Trust. Wanting and needing housing, they did and said what they had to do and say to get housing. They would give me the scoop, including what was going on at the hotel and what the city employees were saying about Take Back the Land and even the Umoja Village itself. Conversely, the Trust could never seem to find rooms for the most ardent and vocal defenders of the Village.

The decision to politicize the placement of residents not only harmed the residents, but the Trust itself. The residents could feel the tension, even if they could not articulate it, and, in the end, they lost respect for the Trust and felt little obligation towards them. Consequently, there were some rough nights at that hotel.

Eventually, we realized they were not serious about housing our residents, and so we had to do it ourselves—again. The unhoused, and even some of the housed, residents wanted to stick together and maintain the family we built, another testament to the power of Umoja. However, given the settlement and other factors, we were not prepared to build another shantytown, even though some residents began lobbying in favor of the idea.

I contacted one of our strongest supporters, who offered his warehouse for use as a temporary shelter. Ten or so residents moved into an abandoned warehouse a dozen blocks from the land. The sense of unity and camaraderie was awesome to witness, and the singular central location allowed us to continue to accept donations. However, the conditions there were not good and it was difficult to watch people you care for living on blanket-covered concrete floors, with minimal lighting and inadequate air circulation.

Because the warehouse was not covered under Pottinger, we were putting both the residents at risk for living there and the owner at risk for housing them. Therefore, the rules there were strict. The circumstances took their toll on the residents who yearned for the freedom they enjoyed at Umoja.

As bad as things were there, more people came to live there than left to go elsewhere. One person, tired of the nightly disruptions and antics, left the city-provided hotel and moved into the warehouse. Also, because the city used its entire allotment of rooms on the Umoja residents, the Trust began dropping homeless people, including those with no relation to Umoja, at the warehouse! We were compelled to inform the Trust that we were not running a shelter.

Because we provided food on a daily basis at the warehouse, the Trust often picked up their hotel residents and dropped them at the warehouse for a meal. Knowing they were talking bad about us at night and then eating into our food supply during the day caused a great deal of friction, but we did not turn anyone away unless they were unruly and, therefore, threatened our existence there.

As we knew it would, the arrangement eventually ended. After two months, we cleared out and left the warehouse, under stress and a sense of panic and loss. The residents who decided to stick together—a group of about 10—began living in adjoining empty lots close to Umoja.

Exacerbating matters, the Liberty City Trust consistently sought to end their responsibilities towards the residents. After we left the warehouse, I warily returned to the Trust to reiterate our housing demands, but was told that since they dispersed from the warehouse, the residents were now "individuals" and no longer a "group." Because the Trust agreed to house the "group" of Umoja residents, it claimed to have no responsibilities towards these individuals. My jaw dropped.

I rounded up as many residents as I could, and, at 4:50PM, brought ten frustrated and angry homeless people to the Liberty City Trust office, told them what was said, pointed to the office door and left.

Half an hour later, I received a call informing me that the Trust "found" a new service provider and set up an intake meeting for early the following week.

After months of thought, research and meetings, we completed our development proposal. We partnered with Carrfour Supportive Housing as the developer and Neighbors And Neighbors Association (NANA) as the small business organization. While we devised a basic outline, the details—such as what kinds of businesses were needed, how many stories high, how many bedrooms should each unit contain, etc., and other questions—were left to our outreach process, during which the community would shape the final look and composition of the development.

Completing the proposal was quite a challenge for us because we had to learn basic principles of development in order to properly serve our community. We researched other projects, particularly the ownership schemes, ultimately settling on a land trust.

In the process, I realized it would be more difficult than I initially anticipated for me to drop out of the development phase and resume my oppositional political work, a prospect which stressed me deeply.

The work was tedious and, at times, frustrating, but in early July, we submitted our proposal to Commissioner Spence-Jones for inclusion in the July City Commission meeting. We named the development Umoja Rising.

THE "DOUBLE REVERSE END AROUND BACK TO THE OTHER SIDE" TRICK PLAY

After submitting the proposal, we sought confirmation the item would appear on the July 26 City of Miami Commission agenda, as the board does not meet in August. Days later, Spence-Jones herself e-mailed to inform me "the land will go out for bid," a complete and unacceptable change from the direct conveyance agreement we agreed upon.

The sudden shift in the city's position was problematic in many respects, including our ability to quickly respond to the turn of events. In the months following the fire, Take Back the Land demobilized to focus on internal organizational structure, the status of the residents and developing the proposal. We did not engage in any media—the *Miami*

Times, the local black press, questioned why we were so quiet—and put our many supporters on ice.

While Umoja was up and running, we represented a powerful political force in the community. After the fire, we represented a threat as we planned our week of action. Evidently, the city reassessed the situation, and surmised that since we were demobilized and out of the news, we were no longer serious concern to them. Consequently, while it made perfect sense to placate us in April by offering us the land, in their minds, the conditions on the ground had changed so significantly by July, there was no reason at all for them to follow through on their promises, which were made publicly and openly. For her part, Spence-Jones claimed that she never actually said she would give us the land, if only we had listened carefully enough to her words.

Needless to say, the residents were furious and most of their comments were far too vulgar to reprint here. Instead of bringing supporters to the July 26 City Commission meeting, we prepared to mobilize protests, and possibly arrests, instead. We were forced back into war mode.

Two days before the big showdown, our mutual friend paid me another visit, bringing news from the Commissioner. Spence-Jones wanted to meet to discuss her new proposal, which would make us all very happy. Amanda was so distrustful of Spence-Jones, she demanded the right to video tape the meeting, but settled on taking real time notes on her laptop.

When we arrived at her office, Spence-Jones informed Mamyrah, Amanda, T-bone and myself that her intention, the entire time, was to keep the process transparent. As such, she was not able to respond to our repeated requests for clarifications and assurances over the course of the previous two weeks. It was for our own good.

She then provided us with her assessment of our opposition to winning the land, the vast majority of which emanated from the Emergency Housing Task Force, a task force she convened herself, specifically for the purpose of opposing the Umoja Village. She informed us that we also faced opposition from the Homeless Trust, particularly its powerful chair, the ethically-challenged lobbyist Ron Book.

Spence-Jones went on to explain that this sizable opposition was precisely the reason she was forced, two weeks prior, to publicly say she would put the land to bid. She wanted to make certain the opposition did not have the opportunity to mobilize their forces against us. Now that she successfully de-mobilized our opposition, Spence-Jones announced to us that she was putting the proposal to convey us the land back on the City Commission agenda, just as she had planned all along.

So, the reason she went back on her commitment to give us the land, was so that she could give us the land. Aha!

Unfortunately for us, instead of investing the past two weeks to turn out our supporters, as we planned, we were forced to mobilize a protest against the Commission meeting. Now, it looked as if we would have to cancel our protest. We bit our tongues, sat on our hands and rode out the remainder of the meeting.

We were frustrated at the turn of events, but more importantly afraid to cancel the protest and face another change of plans. Our people were understandably upset at Spence-Jones and Mayor Manny Diaz, who, surely, was pulling strings behind the scene. Nonetheless, we met, discussed the new situation and resolved to focus on the July 26th Commission meeting first and then deal with the other issues afterwards.

As we evaluated our position, we recognized that our opposition on the Emergency Housing Task Force was in a political jam because, given our level of community support, they could not afford to oppose us openly. That left us with the infamous Ron Book. While Book and I did not get along well, our direct interaction with each other was limited enough that we lacked real acrimony between us. I did have a good working relationship with David Raymond, the Director of the Homeless Trust, so I reached out to him directly in order to understand his perspective and we engaged in a frank and informative discussion.

Because the Homeless Trust seemed to have no direct interest in a deal between Take Back the Land, the City of Miami and the Liberty City community, we decided that the opposition from Book was one of the issues with which we would deal after the July 26th meeting. The residents clowned me for agreeing to meet with the suits.

On July 26th, we arrived at the Commission chambers just before 5:00PM and waited until our item was called, shortly after 11:00PM. We said a few words, and the Commissioners lavished praise upon us. It was a bit uncomfortable, to say the least.

That night, the Commission voted 4-0 for the agenda item and ordered the city manager to hammer out the details required for direct conveyance of land, without a bid, to the partnership headed by Serve the People, Inc. Commission ordinances require two readings, so six days later, on August 1, the Commission would take their final vote on the matter.

We sat in stunned silence. Spence-Jones looked at us in the front row and insisted "you won, you can be happy." By virtually any standard, it was an amazing turn of events. Less than one year ago, we seized public land and were nearly arrested, but on Thursday, July 26, 2007, the City of Miami Commission voted 4-0 to give us that land.

The very next day the entire deal was dead.

ANATOMY OF A DEAL BREAKER

The morning after the vote, our development partner, Carrfour, called anxious about Ron Book. In addition to being the most powerful lobbyist in the state of Florida, Book is the chair of the Homeless Trust, which funds all agencies in the county working on homelessness, including Carrfour.

In a determined effort to block this historic victory and dismantle the previous night's vote, Book was busy calling officials at the city and the county the next day, possibly even earlier than that. He enlisted the support and assistance of several big hitters, including the county manager, who, among other acts, refused to include the county land parcels in the deal, making the deal far less attractive.

Book is the prototype insider lobbyist, securing back room deals that help him and his clients, often with horrific results for the general public. When corporate interests want something done in Florida, and they know their proposal is a loser, they hire Ron Book. No one knows for sure how he closes those deals, but I would venture to guess that ethical constraints are not a major roadblock to his success.

In addition to lobbying for corporations, Book is the lobbyist of choice for cities and counties across Florida, who hire him to lobby state officials on their behalf. Book is the official lobbyist for the cities of North Miami, North Miami Beach and, of course, Miami, as well as Miami-Dade County and a dozen other municipalities.

That means Book simultaneously lobbies both to and for government bodies, lobbying officials on behalf of corporations one day and representing those same officials the next. It should come as no surprise, then, to learn that Book contributes to and raises money for virtually every sitting elected official, often contributing to multiple candidates in the same race, just to be sure. The stories of unethical lobbyists simultaneously representing both sides of a dispute is child's play for Book, who once represented all three sides of a three-sided dispute.

On the Umoja land deal, Book worked his magic in three ways: first, he used his connections and inside information to advance his position with City and County Commissioners, the county manager and others. Second, he implied funding cuts for Carrfour if they remained in the partnership, putting Carrfour in the position of choosing between a group reviled in the halls of power and the man who approves their operational budget. And third, Book announced that if the land deal passed, the Trust would not sign off on our tax credit application.

Because rents on the proposed development had to be low enough to accommodate the residents of Umoja Village, we could not just get a $24 million mortgage to pay for construction. Carrfour planned to utilize state tax credits, a common financing scheme in which corporations purchase tax credits and the funds are used to build very low-income housing. Carrfour anticipated attracting about $20 million in tax credits, leaving a more manageable $4 million to finance in other ways. This financing plan would allow the units to be rented to very low income residents.

However, a prerequisite of the tax credit application is the inclusion of the project in the local homeless "continuum of care." Signing the one page letter would cost the Homeless Trust nothing, as the program itself is run by the state. However, because the Continuum of Care letter is a requirement for the tax-credit application, the Trust's refusal to sign precluded the development from consideration for the $20 million in financing.

Given the high profile nature of this deal, losing our development partner was no major obstacle, as we were practically beating away unsolicited offers from companies looking to partner with us. So, if Carrfour chose to leave, we could find a replacement development partner. However, our inability to secure tax credit financing meant we could build nothing, regardless of who partnered with us.

For the record, none of the principals in Take Back the Land, Serve the People, Carrfour or NANA, our small business development partner, had any intention of living in the proposed housing. Killing the deal, therefore, primarily hurt our residents and other low income people who might have benefited from the development, the very people the Homeless Trust is charged to help.

After discussing the latest developments, we realized that Carrfour would have no choice but to drop out of the project. From the beginning, our disposition was one of non-desperation and a willingness to give up the deal before compromising our principles or dignity. Therefore, we had nothing to lose by exposing Ron Book and his phony moral stance. We would win or lose fighting, not begging.

Book justified his opposition to the deal by asserting that direct conveyance of government land was bad government, and that all such deals should go through a bid process. Therefore, the Homeless Trust would withhold its support and resources, thereby killing the deal. The argument, of course, was nothing but a cynical load of crap.

Aside from the fact that the land belonged neither to Book nor the Trust, the public policy implications of his position were significant. His actions meant that any unelected board of a government agency could veto decisions made by the elected officials for whom the board works. In addition to gutting the power of elected officials, what happens if and when two different agencies, unilaterally and in secret, adopt opposing priorities? How do elected officials resolve the opposing mandates from their underlings? Further, if this power were granted to agencies, no one in their right mind would ever run for public office knowing that the real power lay in the hands of the unelected boards of government agencies. This application of Book's doctrine was particularly flawed because in this instance the board preparing to overturn the Commission's vote did not even oversee an agency of the city, but an agency of the county.

Pubic policy implications aside, the merits of his argument demanded that we discover if he was asserting a principled position, or if Book ever lobbied for a no-bid deal himself.

We planned to publish a position paper on Book's actions and Amanda argued for an unemotional relay of the facts. Amanda researched feverishly, and the more she learned about Book the more disgusted with him she became.

Mamyrah researched the clients for whom Book lobbied before the state, information which is public record because it involves elected officials, although Book is leading the fight to keep such information secret. Our research paid off as we uncovered countless instances of unethical, and illegal, behavior and numerous instances in which Book lobbied on behalf of no-bid deals, of which two instances were particularly pertinent.

The non-profit organization JESCA annually receives hundreds of thousands of dollars in no-bid contracts, and still receives funding from Book and the Trust, in spite of severe mismanagement at the hands of their director, and sell-out County Commissioner, Dorrin Rolle. Why is Book unconcerned by JESCA's ongoing no-bid arrangement with the county? Perhaps it is because Rolle, in his capacity as a Commissioner, voted to hire Book as a lobbyist for Miami-Dade County. So Rolle pays Book from County funds and Book pays Rolle from the Trust funds.

In the other instance, the non-profit organization New Horizons received, in February 2006—less than six months previous—free and without a bid, land and an apartment building, with ground floor commercial space, on the corner of 12th Avenue and 60th Street, just seven blocks from the Umoja Village, from the City of Miami. While the New Horizons deal sounds similar to the Umoja deal, Book raised no objection to the New Horizons deal and continued to fund the agency through the Homeless Trust, including tens of thousands of dollars for a supportive housing facility in the no-bid building.

Why did Book fail to evoke his principled stance against no-bid deals? Perhaps it is because Book was the paid lobbyist for New Horizons. New Horizons pays Book $40,000 a year to lobby the state government, which is in session three months out of the year, and Book approves New Horizons' funding through the Trust.

The residents were furious at the news, and more than one opined that Book, a rich and powerful white man, simply did not want to see poor black people organized and acquiring land. We forwarded the information to a Miami Herald reporter who agreed to cover the story in time for the second and decisive Commission meeting. We depended on the story to expose Book and, therefore, to give us ground under which we could fight the battle in the minds of the public, even if we had no chance of winning before the City Commission. Instead, the reporter effectively killed the story, running it the day after the Commission meeting, just in time to be of use to no one at all.

As expected, Carrfour dropped out of the partnership. During the August 1st Commission meeting, we leveled our criticisms of the process and answered questions. Commissioner Tomas Regalado, who also sits on the Homeless Trust board, delivered an insightful and thoughtful history and perspective of the bad blood between Take Back the Land and Ron Book. In the end, the Commission did not give us the land, instead putting it out for bid, and mandated unspecified participation and inclusion of the Umoja Village residents.

Under other circumstances, compelling a municipality to both put land out for bid under a specific development framework and mandating the participation of a grassroots organization might qualify as a victory. However, given our political orientation towards the adversarial possession of land as a path towards liberation, Take Back the Land is not suited or inclined towards the bid process. While there is nothing inherently wrong with bidding on land, it is difficult to build a movement rooted in the RFP and bidding process. Therefore, we did not participate in the subsequent bid for the land on which the Umoja Village sat.

Ultimately, the deal was blocked by the powers, the real powers, not because the system is against no-bid deals, but because it is against black working class communities building their own power and controlling their own land.

It is important to understand the political settlement in its historic and political context. Those in power consistently lecture the black community about improving our collective lot by engaging the system, wielding our power and working hard to convince or compel city hall to heed our demands. That is exactly what we did.

Make no mistake, this settlement was historic and marked a rare occasion in which progressive forces beat the system. After seizing control of the land and building the Umoja Village, local governments actively sought to eliminate our settlement, to no avail. Consequently, the city struck a political settlement in which they traded an acre of land, and possibly some cash, in exchange for an end to the shantytown.

We developed and presented a proposal, and the officials entrusted with making decisions on behalf of the city agreed to the proposal. Based on their own self-interest, city leaders deemed the deal a good one. From the community's perspective, we took control of land in our community and then won that land.

We worked the system and we won. Which is exactly why the real powers had to change the rules.

CIRCUIT BREAKERS

Outlets are designed to give power to single appliances or electronics. The power demands associated with plugging multiple appliances into a single outlet, however, would overwhelm that outlet, threatening the entire power system.

To defend itself from those demands, power systems distribute outlets throughout the home or office and strategically employ circuit breakers to act as secondary defense systems. When outlets are overwhelmed, the circuit breakers kick in, overriding and shutting down individual outlets as a means of protecting the power system itself.

To accomplish standard tasks, such as lighting a room, watching TV or cooling off, we interact with the outlets. On occasion, we even change the outlets, although, most of the time, the change is superficial, merely replacing one faceplate with another.

When that outlet is overwhelmed, however, the circuit breakers take control and it is made perfectly clear that the outlets are not the real source of power. While the majority of our interactions with power is on the level of the outlet, in order to fundamentally impact where and how power is distributed, addressing the outlets is woefully insufficient.

The City of Miami was overwhelmed by Umoja Village. To be sure, it was not overwhelmed by Umoja alone, as years of public corruption, ongoing community organizing and the severity of the housing crisis all played roles in overwhelming the local outlets of power. But the end result was that the city was forced to make a deal that was previously unthinkable: give land to the collective black community, instead of wealthy white developers, in exchange for a cessation of hostilities.

While the settlement made perfect sense in the context of the self-interest of the City of Miami, the interests of the broader power system were drastically different. The city was concerned about the support Umoja was building and their own inability to dictate the terms of our occupation on the land, two concerns which were largely resolved by the settlement. By contrast, the broader power system evidently worried that the deal did not represent a settlement to end one shantytown, but rather a precedent which would inspire and initiate countless more.

So, while the settlement was good for the city, and potentially great for the movement, the implications of the settlement disturbed the real social and economic powerhouses.

The stakes were so high. and the situation so unusual, that a real schism developed among the powers grappling with how to resolve the situation. While the majority of the powers at the city level were willing to quell the uprising by giving land to a burgeoning movement, others were determined to crush manifestations of black self-determination, thereby preventing the potential expansion and exportation of a real Black Power land movement. The two responses to the crisis were so fundamentally different that only one could prevail.

In the end, Miami Commissioners simply did not have enough power to implement their own settlement, involving the land they ostensibly owned and controlled. Consequently, after the community won its battle against the public face of power—the elected officials—the circuit breakers of the power system kicked in and killed the deal.

The City of Miami voted to disburse their own land, ethically, legally and openly, and the power system's circuit breakers, led by a rich and powerful lobbyist, overturned the decision made by the elected officials of a sovereign municipal government.

THE NEXT STEP

There is no way to sugarcoat the loss of the Umoja Village. The land we controlled for just over six months is now out of our control, a tremendous defeat for the community and the movement. Our efforts to take full and legal control over the land also ended in failure. However, none should confuse the killing of a deal with the killing of a movement.

Umoja not only forged a model for the adversarial takeover of land, but also established a potential conclusion to the struggle: community ownership of that land.

More importantly, the principles that guided our decision to found the Umoja Village in the first place—land, self-determination, the need for housing, etc.—are just as valid today as they were on October 23, 2006. In some respects, even more so.

At this writing, local governments here continue to resist mightily the demands to build low-income housing. Shady back room deals result in more pork projects and boondoggles, but not more housing or jobs for the black community. Local and federal governments, in the meantime, are breaking their necks to bail out the speculators who lost on their gamble.

In addition, as the economic pendulum swings in the other direction, Miami-Dade county is the epicenter of the housing bust, resulting in tens of thousands of homes becoming vacant due to record foreclosures; while tens of thousands of high-priced condos are being completed, but will likely stand brand new and unoccupied. Tragically and ironically, but not surprisingly, as more people become homeless or underhoused, more homes are becoming vacant.

Recognizing the potential to make money when they see it, wealthy speculators and developers lie in wait to snatch up the foreclosures and restart the cycle of gentrification again. These vulture capitalists profit handsomely off of the misery of the masses in an immoral and unethical, but perfectly legal, manner.

Some people own five, six, even ten or more pairs of shoes, some of which are worn only once a year, at weddings or other rare occasions. While such a practice is perfectly acceptable in the context of shoes, it is not in the context of land and housing. While multitudes are homeless, a small number of wealthy individuals own multiple lots of land and housing, some of which remain vacant for long stretches at a time.

In addition, most of the land in black communities is not controlled by those communities, a dynamic which contributes to our tenuous grip on even the tiniest bits of power, and the reason why others are able to impose systems of segregation and gentrification upon us.

We assert that housing is a human right, not a privilege, and, therefore, every human is entitled to decent housing. Furthermore, one person's right to housing supersedes another's right to make a profit.

Because the crisis of gentrification and housing persists, our core mission and strategies remain relevant and viable. Consequently, immediately after losing the land, Take Back the Land began the tedious process of identifying vacant public housing units and foreclosed homes. In October 2007, we liberated a foreclosed home and moved a homeless family into a family-less home. We have been identifying units and moving in families ever since.

Epilogue

SO THIS IS THE story of the Umoja Village. However, to be clear, the Umoja Village is but one small piece of a larger puzzle, a larger story and struggle: the story and struggle of oppressed people for control over land.

Therefore, the point of this epilogue is identical to the point of the prologue: to reiterate that the situation and struggle in which we are engaged is not fundamentally about gentrification or segregation, but rather, it is fundamentally about collective control over land.

This concept is important not only in contextualizing the political existence and significance of the Umoja Village, but also in developing the road map forward. Understanding land as the fundamental issue underlying the surface problems associated with gentrification is critical to devising a strategy to confront and defeat gentrification itself.

Equally as important, many recognize this was neither the first, nor the last, round of forced dislocation, as gentrification is a cyclical economic phenomenon, inherent in economic systems that allow both the private ownership of the earth and fantastic wealth for those who produce nothing more than insightful speculation.

The notion of land struggle as fundamental takes on greater importance as the current gentrification cycle recedes, and we are forced to ask ourselves what comes next after gentrification? How do we defend our communities against block-busting and capital divestment?

The fact is, by the time many of us started fighting gentrification, the game was already in the fourth quarter. Our people will not be well served by a movement swinging hard towards the shadows of gentrification, while new forms of oppression ravage our fragile communities.

Whatever specific form the next fight takes, the land question remains central to any comprehensive response. As the housing situation deteriorates and the gap between the wealthy and poor grows, shantytowns will spring up across the US, in rural areas in the cities. In fact, they already have. The criminalization of the poor will empower the police to crush attempts to provide basic shelter, but as the number of shantytowns—and their residents—swell, the crackdown will prove futile.

We thank land movements around the world, particularly in South Africa, Brazil and India, for their inspiration, and hope that Umoja Village serves as a model for land struggles in the U.S.

Forward,
Max Rameau

Jerry stops the bulldozer.
Police start mass arrests.

John Cata is arrested and taken into custody.

Jonathan and Micah say goodbye to
the land.

Support AK Press!

AK Press is one of the world's largest and most productive anarchist publishing houses. We're entirely worker-run and democratically man-

aged. We operate without a corporate structure—no boss, no managers, no bullshit. We publish close to twenty books every year, and distribute thousands of other titles published by other like-minded independent presses from around the globe.

The Friends of AK program is a way that you can directly contribute to the continued existence of AK Press, and ensure that we're able to keep publishing great books just like this one! Friends pay a minimum of $25 per month, for a minimum three month period, into our publishing account. In return, Friends automatically receive (for the duration of their membership), as they appear, one free copy of every new AK Press title. They're also entitled to a 20% discount on everything featured in the AK Press Distribution catalog and on the website, and a 50% discount on AK Press-published items, on any and every order.

You or your organization can even sponsor an entire book if you should so choose!

There's great stuff in the works—so sign up now to become a Friend of AK Press, and let the presses roll!

Won't you be our friend? Email friendsofak@akpress.org for more info, or visit the Friends of AK Press website:
http://www.akpress.org/programs/friendsofak